WORLD HISTORY

Observations and Assessments from Creation to Today

James P. Stobaugh

First printing: March 2012

Master Books®, P.O. Box 726, Green Forest, AR 72638

Master Books® is a division of the New Leaf Publishing Group, Inc.

ISBN-13: 978-0-89051-647-8

Cover design by Diana Bogardus.
Interior design by Terry White.

Please consider requesting that a copy of this volume be purchased by your local library system.

Printed in the United States of America

Please visit our website for other great titles:
www.masterbooks.net

For information regarding author interviews, please contact the publicity department at (870) 438-5288

Master Books®
A Division of New Leaf Publishing Group
www.masterbooks.net

This book is dedicated to this new generation of young believers whose fervor and dedication to the purposes of the Lord shall yet bring a great revival. Stand tall, young people, and serve our Lord with alacrity and courage!

HOW TO USE YOUR TEACHER GUIDE

How this course has been developed:

1. **Teacher:** this allows one to study the student objectives with each chapter, providing the answers to the assignments and the weekly exam.

2. **Chapters:** this course has 34 chapters (representing 34 weeks of study).

3. **Lessons:** each chapter has 5 lessons each, taking approximately 20 to 30 minutes each. There will be a short reading followed by critical thinking questions. Some questions require a specific answer from the text where others are more open-ended, leading the student to think "outside the box."

4. **Weekly exams:** the final lesson of the week is the exam covering the week's chapter. Students are not to use their text to answer these questions unless otherwise directed.

5. **Student responsibility:** Responsibility to complete this course is on the student. Students are to complete the readings every day, handing their responses to a parent or teacher for evaluation. Independence is strongly encouraged in this course designed for the student to practice independent learning.

6. **Grading:** A parent or teacher can grade assignments daily or weekly, and keep track of this in their files. Assignments with answers are available at the end of each chapter.

Throughout this book you will find the following components:

1. **Narrative Background:** background on the period.

2. **Critical Thinking Questions:** questions based roughly on Bloom's Taxonomy.

3. **Concepts/Generalizations:** terms, concepts, and theories to be learned.

4. **History Maker:** a person(s) who clearly changed the course of history.

5. **Historiographies or Historical Debate:** an examination of historical theories surrounding a period or topic.

6. **World View Formation:** An overview of historical understandings of who God is. There is also a subsection where we examine important thinkers of the period/topic.

7. **History & World View Overview:** an overview of world views.

What the student will need:

1. **Notepad:** for writing assignments.

2. **Pen/pencil:** for the answers and essays.

3. **Weekly Exams:** available at the back of teacher guide or as a free download at: nlpg.com/worldhistoryexam.

ABOUT THE AUTHOR

James P. Stobaugh and his wife, Karen, have homeschooled their four children since 1985. They have a growing ministry, For Such a Time As This Ministries, committed to challenging this generation to change its world for Christ.

Dr. Stobaugh is an ordained pastor, a certified secondary teacher, and an SAT coach. His academic credentials include: BA, cum laude Vanderbilt University; Teacher Certification, Peabody College for Teachers; MA, Rutgers University; MDiv, Princeton Theological Seminary; Merrill Fellow, Harvard University; DMin Gordon Conwell Seminary.

Dr. Stobaugh has written articles for magazines: *Leadership, Presbyterian Survey, Princeton Spire, Ministries Today,* and *Pulpit Digest.* Dr. Stobaugh's books include the *SAT Preparation Course for the Christian Student,* the *ACT Preparation Course for the Christian Student,* as well as *American History, British History,* and *World History* high school curriculum.

Contents

PREFACE

History is meant to be a light that illuminates the present and directs attention toward the possibilities of the future. However, history is only ancient, dusty chronicles if one does not honestly study and asses these written records of events, as well as the events themselves. History is a social science¾a branch of knowledge that uses specific methods and tools to achieve its goals.

Historians examine archival footprints. Some of these are written records: diaries, letters, oral histories, recordings, inscriptions, biographies, and many others. At times history seems merely to be a list of kings, of wars, and of other significant things. As a result, it can seem like only the study of a bunch of dead people. Who cares? Like Huck Finn, we quip, "After supper the widow Douglas got out her book and learned me about Moses and the bulrushes, and I was in a sweat to find out all about him; but by and by she let it out that Moses had been dead a considerable long time; so then I didn't care no more about him, because I don't take no stock in dead people" (Twain, Mark. The Adventures of Huckleberry Finn).

But history is alive, and full of interesting, glorious, and useful things! And it is terribly relevant to all of us.

There are lots of different histories. The Earth, the world of nature, and the universe all have pasts, but they have no histories, per se. Histories have to do with real, alive (or once alive) people. Only human societies have histories, based on collective memories from which they reconstruct their pasts.

Not all attempts to reconstruct the past have resulted in histories. My Uncle George (not a real uncle but just a family friend), grand wizard of the Ku Klux Klan, had an entirely different view of African history than I, a father of three African-American children. Uncle George had a delusional "history" that was very much like a Nazi propaganda film, but it was not a "history." It was a "past" made up of venal images, obscured remembrances, and visceral prejudices that stewed in his poor, conflicted mind.

My history was big enough to love Uncle George—may he rest in peace—and I did, as did my three children. And in my life, we were brought together into an eternal peace. Perhaps that is the best thing one can say about world history; it brings everyone together in one shared history.

To be a true history, an account of the past must not only retell what happened but must also relate events and people to each other. It must inquire into causes and effects. It must try to discern falsehood in the old records, such as attempts of historical figures to make them look better than they really

were. It must also present the evidence on which its findings are based.

It is clear that all our information in regard to past events and conditions must be derived from evidence of some kind, and certain evidences are better than others.

To that end, I do not expect students to be completely neutral about historical sources. And yet, scholarly historical inquiry demands that we implement the following principles:

1. Historians must evaluate the veracity of sources. There must be a hierarchy of historical sources. Primary source material, for instance, is usually the best source of information.

2. Historians must be committed to telling both sides of the historical story. They may choose to lobby for one view over the other, but they must fairly examine all theories.

3. Historians must avoid stereotypes and archetypes. They must overcome personal prejudices and dispassionately view history in ruthlessly objective terms.

4. Historians must be committed to the truth no matter where their scholarship leads them. At times historians will discover unflattering information about their nation/state.

5. Finally, historians understand that real, abiding, and eternal history is ultimately made only by people who obey God at all costs.

After everything is said and done, historians are only studying the past. They cannot really change the past. Theories about the past come and go, and change with each generation; however, the past is past. Historians will debate about history, but they can never alter it. Only God can change history, and God alone.

When persons are reborn in Christ, their present, future, and, yes, even their past is changed. History is literarily rewritten. They are new creations. That bad choice, that sin, that catastrophe is placed under the blood of the Lamb, and everything starts fresh and new; a new history for new people.

My prayer is that if you do not know this God who can change history—even your history—this history text might encourage you to invite Jesus Christ into your heart as Savior.

Chapter 1

MESOPOTAMIA

First Thoughts . . .

Authorities in the field of history do not all agree about the definition of civilization. Most accept the view that "a civilization is a culture which has attained a degree of complexity usually characterized by urban life." In other words, a civilization is a culture capable of sustaining the social, political, and religious needs of a densely populated society. The Mesopotamian region, beginning with the Sumerians, created a system of writing to keep records, monumental architecture in place of simple buildings, and art that was worthy of its people. All these characteristics of civilization first appeared in Mesopotamia.

Chapter Learning Objectives . . .

As a result of this chapter you should be able to:

1. Discuss at least three important contributions that the Sumerian civilization made to the Western world.
   Answer Assignment 1

2. Contrast Mesopotamian gods and goddesses with the Jewish God.
   Answer Assignment 2

3. Write a short report on the life of Daniel.
   Answer Assignment 3

4. Analyze the Mesopotamian civilizations.
   Answer Chapter Exam

5. Describe an ordinary day in the life of a 14 to 18-year-old Mesopotamian youth.
   Answer Assignment 4

LESSON 1

THE STORY OF MESOPOTAMIA

Assignment

Discuss at least three important contributions that the Sumerian civilization made to the Western world.

Answer: The Sumerians provided the Western world with the first alphabet, the wheel and the first legal system. Sumerians developed a system of writing by imprinting on clay tablets using a stylus. A form of printing was a similar first: they carved negative images on a stone cylinder usually from two to six centimeters long. These were repeatedly rolled over fresh clay to produce positive inscriptions. As forerunners of finger rings used to imprint wax seals in later times, they were used to identify possessions, to seal written tablets, and to protect other valuables. Sumerians also invented the wheel and therefore improved transportation endeavors and building programs. Finally, Hammurabi's Code was the first legal system that required a society to be founded on a rule of law. Later, of course, Moses was to establish a better code of law with the Ten Commandments.

LESSON 2

MESOPOTAMIA

Assignment

Contrast Mesopotamian gods and goddesses with the Jewish God.

Answer: Mesopotamian religions were polytheistic and limited to their sphere of influence. The Jewish God is one and all-powerful. The Mesopotamian gods were appeased and controlled (presumably) by human actions and appeals. The Jewish God is omnipotent, and, while He is concerned about the morality of His followers, His relationship is based on covenantal contracts. The Jewish God has created mankind in His image; not so with the Mesopotamian gods and goddesses. Finally, the Jewish God cares for, even loves, His people. The Mesopotamian gods and goddesses are not personally involved in the lives of their people.

LESSON 3

HISTORY MAKER: DANIEL

Assignment

Write a short report on the life of Daniel. How is your life similar to and different from the life of Daniel?

Answer: Daniel is the main character of the Book of Daniel in the Old Testament. The name Daniel means "God is my judge." Daniel was carried off to Babylon where he was trained in the service of the court of Nebuchadnezzar.

Assignment

Describe an ordinary day in the life of a 14 to 18-year-old Mesopotamian youth.

Answer: Children were expected to obey their parents in all cases. For example, the spouse of a Sumerian child was chosen by his/her parent. Those children who chose to disobey the authority of their parents faced being disinherited or sold into slavery. The everyday appearance of the Sumerian people was rather simple. The men of Sumer often sported long hair with a part in the middle. Their attire initially consisted of wrap-around skirts and felt cloaks, but it eventually evolved into long skirts accented by large shawls flung over the left shoulder of the wearer. The right shoulder and arm were left bare. Children wore the same clothes as adults. Sumerian women also wore their hair long. Most women would braid their locks into one long braid which they then wrapped around the top of their heads. For clothing, Sumerian women wore long shawls which covered their entire bodies, but their right arm and shoulder would also be left bare. The early Sumerians lived in homes that were built out of reeds. Eventually, homes were constructed of sun-dried mud-bricks, but stone buildings were not erected due to a lack of that resource in the area. Modest homes were usually one-story high with an open court in the center, around which there were several rooms. Wealthy individuals, however, often built homes two stories high with approximately 12 rooms, including servants' quarters (www.msnu.edu).

EXAM KEY

Dates (15 points)

Mark these events in the order in which they occurred:

1   The Sumerians build a city-state.

3   The Jews are taken to Babylon as exiles.

4   The Persians invade Mesopotamia.

5   The Jews rebuild Jerusalem.

2   The Babylonians invade Mesopotamia.

Matching (35 points)

Answer:

A. Persians
B. Sumerians
C. King Cyrus
D. Babylonians
E. Marduk
F. Ziggurats
G. King Sargon I
H. King Nebachunezzar
I. Tigris and Euphrates

I   1. The two rivers around whose fertile soil civilization arose in Mesopotamia.

B   2. The first people to form a city-state, civilization, in Mesopotamia.

G   3. Akkadian king who for the first time in Mesopotamian history united Sumer and Akkad.

D   4. A people group that conquered the Mesopotamia area and built the great city of Babylon.

A   5. Conquered the Babylonians.

F   6. The Sumerian temples whose distinctive features were their height and width.

E   7. The chief Babylonian god.

H   8. This king conquered Jerusalem.

C   9. This king conquered Babylon and allowed the exilic Jews to return home.

Discussion Question (50 points)

Zerubbabel, prince of Judah and governor of Jerusalem, born in Babylon during the captivity. He was a direct descendant of King David (see Ezra 2:2; Haggai 1:1). When King Cyrus permitted the captive Jews in Babylon to return to Judah (538? BC), Zerubbabel led the first contingent, numbering some 42,000. Cyrus appointed him (see Haggai 1:14) secular governor of Jerusalem. There he organized the rebuilding of the temple, which had been destroyed in 586 BC by King Nebuchadnezzar. However, many scholars believe that he resigned his post and returned to Babylon. I think this is true, Zerubbabel returned to captivity. What causes godly, hardworking, committed Christians to abandon the work and return to comfortable captivity?

Answer: "Thy life will I give thee for a prey in all places whither thou goest" (Jeremiah 45:5).

This is the unshakable secret of the Lord to those who trust Him: "I will give thee thy life." What more does a man want than his life? It is the essential thing. "Thy life for a prey" means that wherever you may go, even if it is into hell, you will come out with your life, nothing can harm it. So many of us are caught up in the show of things, not in the way of property and possessions, but of blessings. All these have to go; but there is something grander that never can go—the life that is "hid with Christ in God."

Are you prepared to let God take you into union with Himself, and pay no more attention to what you call the great things? Are you prepared to abandon entirely and let go? The test of abandonment is in refusing to say, "Well, what about this?" Beware of suppositions. Immediately you allow—What about this?—it means you have not abandoned, you do not really trust God. Immediately you do abandon, you think no more about what God is going to do. Abandon means to refuse yourself the luxury of asking any questions. If you abandon entirely to God, He says at once, "Thy life will I give thee for a prey." The reason people are tired of life is because God has not given them anything, they have not got their life as a prey. The way to get out of that state is to abandon to God. When you do get through to abandonment to God, you will be the most surprised and delighted creature on earth; God has got you absolutely and has given you your life. If you are not there, it is either because of disobedience or a refusal to be simple enough.

Chapter 2

FOUNDATIONS OF WORLD VIEWS

First Thoughts . . .

A world view is the way a person sees, understands, and responds to life from the philosophical position he or she embraces as his or her own. World view is a framework that ties everything together and allows people to understand society, the world, and their place in it. A world view helps people make critical decisions that shape our future. A study of world views is at the heart of world history.

Chapter Learning Objectives . . .

As a result of this chapter you should be able to:

1. Evaluate present controversy over the public display of the Ten Commandments.
   Answer Chapter Exam

2. Compare Hammurabi's Code with the Ten Commandments.
   Answer Chapter Exam

3. Examine Jesus' statements about the Ten Commandments.
   Answer Assignment 1

4. Analyze the importance of Hammurabi's Code to history.
   Answer Chapter Exam

5. Evaluate the possible problems and potential advantages that Hammurabi's Code brought to Babylon.
   Answer Assignment 2

6. Discuss the meaning and importance of world view discernment.
   Answer Questions 3-A, 3-B, 3-C

7. Research ways the Bible depicts Nebuchadnezzar.
   Answer Assignment 4

LESSON 1

FOUNDATIONS OF WORLD VIEWS
Assignment

Approximately 1,400 years after God gave Moses the Ten Commandments, Jesus summed them up when He was confronted by the religious leaders of the day:

> "Teacher, which is the greatest commandment in the Law?" Jesus replied: "'Love the Lord your God with all your heart and with all your soul and with all your mind.' This is the first and greatest commandment. And the second is like it: 'Love your neighbor as yourself.' All the Law and the Prophets hang on these two commandments" (Matthew 22:36–40).

Why did Jesus summarize the Ten Commandments in this way?

Answer: A careful reading of Christ's teaching reveals that the first four commandments are contained in the statement: "Love the Lord your God with all your heart and with all your soul and with all your mind." The last six commandments are enclosed in the statement "Love your neighbor as yourself."

LESSON 2

HAMMURABI
Assignment

The notion that laws might supersede the authority of an autocratic leader was a novel idea. What possible problems and potential advantages did Hammurabi's Code bring to Babylon?

Answer: On one hand laws would protect individual rights; on the other hand, the same laws would limit the monarch's rights. This would ultimately be very advantageous to Babylon but no doubt caused some consternation among despotic kings!

WAR OF THE WORLD VIEWS

A. Match each quote with a world view.

A. Existentialism	Feelings are everything. **A**
B. Deism	My god is the rising sun; my goddess, the rising moon. **D**
C. Naturalism	It is true because I said it is true. **A or E**
D. Romanticism	God was here—He set up our great country—but He is gone now. **B**
E. Realism	Only the world around us has any force. **C**

B. True or False

T	1.	Most Americans today are Theists.
F	2.	Most Americans today are Christian Theists.
T	3.	Postmoderns love to play with scientific gadgets but are inherently suspicious of their efficacy.
T	4.	The decade of the 1960s was a triumph of Existentialism.
T	5.	One reason Americans are so open to the gospel is because our culture has become dysfunctional.
F	6.	A perfect example of postmodernism would be Clint Eastwood.
T	7.	*Toy Story* is a perfect example of postmodernism.
F	8.	The best way to convert a Romantic is to hand him a dead squirrel.
T	9.	John Wayne movies are generally Theistic movies.
T	10.	The *Star Wars* movies are Theistic in tone and substance.
T	11.	The Beatles moved from nostalgic Romanticism to nihilistic Absurdism.
T	12.	For most of history, Theism has been the dominant world view.

NEBUCHADNEZZAR

Assignment

Write a report describing how the Bible depicts Nebuchadnezzar.

Answer: Bible teacher Wayne Blank writes: Nebuchadnezzar was the king of the Chaldean (also known as the Neo-Babylonian) Empire. He was born about 630 BC, and died around 562 BC at age 68. He was the most powerful monarch of his dynasty, and is best known for the magnificence of his capital, Babylon . . . his vast military conquests, and his role in Bible history and prophecy. Perhaps surprisingly, his own words are directly recorded in The Bible (Daniel 4:4-18). Nebuchadnezzar was the oldest son of Nabopolassar, the founder of the Chaldean Empire. After serving as commander of the army, Nebuchadnezzar became king upon his father's death in August of 605 BC. By marrying the daughter of Cyaxares, he united the Median and Babylonian dynasties. He wasn't just a warlord, he was also skilled in politics. During Nebuchadnezzar's time, Babylon was the largest city of the world. It has been estimated to have covered over 2,500 acres/1,000 hectares, with the Euphrates River flowing through it. The name of the city came to symbolize the entire empire.

Nebuchadnezzar is best known to students of the Bible for his defeat of the southern kingdom of Judah (the northern kingdom of Israel was by then long gone, having been conquered and deported over a century earlier by the Assyrians . . . By 586 BC, the Babylonian forces conquered the land, devastated Jerusalem, looted and burned the original temple that had been built by Solomon . . . and took the people away into what became known as the "Babylonian Exile" (2 Kings 25:1–17). As powerful as Nebuchadnezzar was, he did not conquer the people of Judah of himself. God didn't just allow it to happen, He actually brought it about (2 Chronicles 36:15–20). The people had become extremely corrupt and idolatrous. They ignored all of the prophets that God had sent to warn them (2 Chronicles 36:15–16), and they refused to repent. They trusted in themselves, in the city of Jerusalem, even in the physical temple, rather than in the Lord Himself. So, God, through Nebuchadnezzar, destroyed it all in order to make them realize, in no uncertain terms, that they had turned their backs on Him.

Among the Jews who were deported from Judah to Babylon was a certain young man known as Daniel. From him, and the Bible book that carries his name, we get some of the most sensational prophecies for our time now.

EXAM KEY

Discussion Question (50 points each)

A. Recently, there has been much debate about whether or not the Ten Commandments should be exhibited in government buildings. State both sides of the argument and offer your own conclusions (50 points).

Answer: Two false assumptions are behind the idea that the Ten Commandments should be removed from public buildings: 1. that America is a secular state, 2. that the Ten Commandments are religious. America may be a secular country today, but originally it was founded as a "city on a hill" (John Winthrop) with a holy purpose. Also, if the Ten Commandments are removed from public buildings, then likewise the Declaration of Independence and the U.S. Constitution—both Judeo-Christian documents—have to be removed.

B. Compare Hammurabi's Code with the Ten Commandments.

Answer: There is nothing about honoring a deity in Hammurabi's Code. That of course is the primary commandment in the Ten Commandments.

Chapter 3

THE JEWISH EXILE

First Thoughts . . .

Nebuchadnezzar, the greatest of Babylonian kings, destroys Israel and takes 10,000 of the most important Jewish leaders back to Babylon. The destruction of the temple and the exile to Babylon represents a tremendous shock to the Jewish people. It may be hard to imagine today what it must have meant back then, because we really have no basis of comparison. Before the Exile, Judaism meant living with the constant presence of God, which was always accessible at the Temple. Miracles occurred near the temple daily and could be witnessed by anyone. For example, whichever way the wind was blowing, the smoke of the sacrifices always went straight to heaven (aish.com). No wonder they wept by the rivers of Babylon. However, while the Babylonians could be very cruel in their conquests, their attitude toward the exiled Jewish community was "live and let live." Life in Babylonia turned out not to be too awful. In fact, by the time Nehemiah was ready to return with a remnant, a majority of Jews preferred to stay in Babylon.

Chapter Learning Objectives . . .

As a result of this chapter you should be able to:

1. Discuss how the covenant theme was a significant part of early Jewish history.
   Answer Assignment 1

2. Evaluate the reasons a majority of Jewish exiles remained in Babylon.
   Answer Questions 2-A

3. Identify ways Christians today can survive and even prosper without being absorbed by the culture surrounding them.
   Answer Questions 2-B

4. Compare and contrast Zoroastrianism with Judaism.
   Answer Assignment 3

5. Define "syncretism" and reframe it as a problem Christians face all the time.
   Answer Chapter Exam

LESSON 1

THE HISTORY OF ISRAEL

Assignment

Discuss how the covenant theme was a significant part of early Jewish history.

Answer: The concept of covenant is central to a basic understanding Scripture. In Old Testament times this complex concept was the foundation of social order and social relations, and it was particularly the foundation for an understanding of humanity's relationship with God. The two were interrelated. For instance, Abram made a covenant with his God that was eternal and irrevocable. Likewise, Moses brought the Ten Commandments (covenant) down from Mt. Sinai. These are core truths of Judaism.

LESSON 2

THE HISTORY OF ISRAEL

Assignment

A. When we read the book of Nehemiah, it's easy to imagine that the majority of Jewish exiles returned to Jerusalem with Nehemiah and Ezra. In fact, though, the majority of Jewish exiles remained in Babylon. Why?

Answer: The Babylonian exile lasted from 586–538 BC. "Exile" means that they were forced to live outside of the Promised Land. Babylon had replaced Assyria as the reigning world power after defeating Egypt at the battle of Carchemish in 609 BC. They conquered Jerusalem in 586. This was the main exile of Israel when the Temple was flattened and Jerusalem was destroyed. These deportations from the Promised Land actually began under the Assyrians as early as 733. These were deported to Nineveh. More deportations to Babylon occurred in 605, 597, and 582. Many of the Israelites had chosen to flee voluntarily and had settled in Syria, Egypt, and Turkey. This was a very dark period in the history of Israel. There was no king and no temple. (See Psalm 137.) The Books of I and II Kings were written about the period leading up to the Babylonian exile to show the people how their plight was the result of Israel's sin. The Book of Daniel is the only record of Israel's time in Babylon. While the first half of Daniel is considered historical, it speaks only about Daniel and his experiences there. It is a theological work, not a history book. He had been a relative of King Zedekiah and was stationed in the royal court of Nebuchadnezzar. All that we have from the exile is what Daniel tells us about the king and what went on in the palace.

Daniel rose quickly in rank while serving the king and eventually rose to a position where he oversaw the whole empire. Stories like Daniel in the Lions' Den and Shadrach, Meshach, and Abednego (the three men who survived the furnace), were meant to inspire the Jews to remain true to their faith. Daniel and the three young men did and God protected them. Jeremiah's prophecy ends with the capture of Jerusalem, and Lamentations is a description of a desolate Jerusalem after the armies of Babylon have plundered and destroyed it. There wasn't any writing or prophesy during the exile. Conservative theologians date Daniel as having been written in Babylon, but later investigation has revealed that Daniel was probably the last Old Testament book written, as late as 137. In 539 Persia replaced Babylon as the new dominant empire. They did not believe in exile, but in resettlement. King Cyrus of Persia decreed that any Jews who wanted to return to Jerusalem and rebuild the temple could do so. The Books of Ezra and Nehemiah record the returns of exiles from Babylon to Israel. The first return occurred in 538 under the leadership of Zerubbabel. Ezra gave the exact numbers of returnees as 42,360 Jews with 7,337 servants and 200 singers. They were listed by "clans" in Ezra 2. They also brought back horses, mules, camels, donkeys, and gold and silver vessels. The temple was rebuilt under Zerubbabel. The prophets Haggai and Zechariah were writing during this period. Zerubbabel seemed slow to rebuild and Haggai spurred him on. Another return took place when Ezra went to Jerusalem with 1,754 males and some gold and silver. The other significant return spoken of in the Bible was Nehemiah. Nehemiah got an armed escort to bring him safely to Jerusalem. He was there to be the governor and to fortify the city. Unfortunately, though, many, if not most, of the Jewish exiles stayed in Mesopotamia. Why? By that point the Jewish community had assimilated into Babylonian/Persian society. Persecutions were over. Families had become productive members of society. Things were not great, but tolerable. This was better though than returning to Palestine and possibly losing everything!

B. Daniel and Esther were called to survive and to prosper in an inhospitable land. Each was a captive of a repressive regime and was asked to be a leader in that regime. Like Daniel and Esther, how can Christians today survive and even prosper without being absorbed by the culture surrounding them?

Answer: Christians must learn to be in a culture, but not of that culture. Like Daniel, Christians must learn to prosper in Babylon without becoming Babylonian. How? Answers will vary. But Daniel was motivated by the Word of God and not by circumstances or feelings. He was respectful to authority but would not disobey the Word of God, even if it put him in harm's way. Likewise, Esther risked everything to save her people. She was willing to lose her anonymity and to take a stand if God asked her to do so.

LESSON 3
ZOROASTRIANISM

Assignment

Compare and contrast Zoroastrianism and Judaism.

Answer: The present world is where good and evil are mixed. People's good works are seen as gradually transforming the world toward its heavenly ideal. Judaism understood that God is wholly good, the devil is wholly bad. Good works are important, but God alone brings transformation. In the future, a final state will occur when good and evil will be separated. In Judaism, they were never together! Both faiths are dualistic—but the Jewish

God is omnipotent, all powerful. He is far more powerful than any evil entity or source. There is no comparison. Eventually, everything will be purified. Even the occupants of hell will be released. Not so in Judaism. A savior will be born of a virgin, but of the lineage of the Prophet Zoroaster, who will raise the dead and judge everyone in a final judgment. A Savior would come, but He would be of the lineage of David.

LESSON 4

JERUSALEM
Assignment

Summarize the history of Jerusalem.

Answer: Jerusalem itself was captured by King David in 1000 BC and called by him "City of David." In 587 BC Jerusalem was destroyed by the Babylonian King Nebuchadnezzar and the temple torn down. In 537 BC Jewish exiles rebuilt the second temple on the ruins of the first. In 333 BC Alexander the Great captured Jerusalem; after his death it fell under the rule of the Egyptians then the Syrians. When Antiochus Epiphanes, in 169 BC, tried to enforce the worship of Greek gods, the Jews, under the leadership of Judas Maccabeus, rebelled and Jerusalem was freed. In AD 66 the Jews revolted and captured the city from the Romans. They held on until AD 70 when Titus destroyed the city and the temple, leaving only the supporting wall, now known as the Western or Wailing Wall. After the Bar Kochba revolt in AD 135, the Roman general Hadrian rebuilt Jerusalem. Queen Helena, Constantine's mother, visited Jerusalem in AD 326, built a church on the site of the crucifixion, and made the city the center of Christianity.

Islamic people conquered the city in AD 637, and built the Dome of the Rock on the Temple Mount, the site of the first and second temples. Jerusalem remained under the rule of Islam until the Crusaders captured it in 1099. In 1187, Jerusalem was occupied by Saladin. In 1229, the Crusaders retook the city, finally sealing its walls in 1244. After a short period of Mongol domination, the Turks captured the city in 1517 and built the walls that still stand today. In December 1917 during World War I, Jerusalem was occupied by British troops. In 1947 the UN recommended that Palestine be divided into a Jewish state and a Palestinian state. The plan was rejected and on the 14th of May 1948, war broke out between the Jews and the Arabs. Jerusalem was declared the official capital of Israel in 1950. The Palestinians also consider Jerusalem to be their capital. The Old City remained in Jordanian hands for 19 years until the Six-Day war in 1967 when it was recaptured by the Israeli forces.

EXAM KEY

Questions: 100-150 Words (100 points)

One problem the Jewish exiles encountered in Babylon was "syncretism." Define this term and discuss why it is a problem Christians face all the time.

Answer: Syncretism is the attempt to reconcile contrary beliefs. Christians do this when they combine their faith with worldly agendas. For a more complete answer to this question, see Lesson 2, B.

Chapter 4

EGYPT

First Thoughts . . .

Perhaps no civilization has captured the imagination more than Egypt. We will travel back in time to a place that has left its imprint and impact on humanity forever. We will discover anew the civilization of Egypt, whose quest for immortality has mystified generations. At no other period of known history has a civilization left behind so many interesting riddles. Why did these people build pyramids? What did they write about the afterlife?

Chapter Learning Objectives . . .

As a result of this chapter you should be able to:

1. Compare the rise of the Egyptian civilization with the rise of the Sumerian civilization.
    Answer Assignment 1

2. Give an overview of the way pyramids were made.
    Answer Assignment 2

3. Describe three of the most important Egyptian pharaohs.
    Answer Assignment 3

4. Discuss why Cleopatra got involved in the Roman Civil War (after the assassination of Julius Caesar).
    Answer Assignment 4

5. Explore the most enduring legacy of Egyptian history.
    Answer Chapter Exam

LESSON 1

ANCIENT EGYPT

Assignment

Compare the rise of the Egyptian civilization with the rise of the Sumerian civilization.

Answer: Both were centered on a river delta location. Egypt had a more defensible position. Sumeria was located at the crossroads between conquerors in the north and south. Both developed writing and complicated religions. The religions, however, were significantly different. Egyptian religions emphasized the afterlife more than the Sumerian religions. All Sumerian religions were polytheistic. Egyptian religions were usually polytheistic, yet there was at least one that was monotheistic. Both civilizations emphasized education and women were treated about the same in both.

LESSON 2

PYRAMIDS AND KINGDOMS

Assignment

Give an overview of the way pyramids were built.

Answer: It required a lot of planning to build such large and complicated structures. Normally, a tertiary director or project manager coordinated the whole project. He would gather a team of engineers and thousands of workers/slaves to help him. No one knows how many workers it took to build a pyramid, but presumably it took a lot. The first task for the engineers was to estimate the amount of stone needed, then to have the stone cut from local quarries. Large sandstone blocks were used for the interior, with limestone on the exterior. Limestone was especially suited for the task. Limestone in its natural state is pliable and soft but hardens on exposure to air. As soon as the limestone was quarried, it was laid out in the desert to cure and harden in the hot, dry air. As soon as a block was cut, it was pushed out using large, smooth beams rolling on rocks to the work site. Often the biggest problem for the workers was not starting the process—it was stopping the process! Going downhill, the blocks could easily accelerate out of control. They had to be manipulated by ropes held around stout anchor poles imbedded in the ground. The blocks could also be pulled up a gentle rise with ease by a team of oxen. Workers built upward from each new base, similar to the way construction crews build skyscrapers today.

GREEK AND ROMAN CONQUEST

Assignment

Describe three of the most important Egyptian pharaohs.

Answer: In 1279–1213 BC, Ramses II began ambitious building projects, including his mortuary temple, the Ramesseum (on the West Bank near Luxor). Many scholars believe that he used the exilic, captive Hebrews as laborers. It was probably from Ramses II that Moses, had freed the Israelites. In an effort to wrest political and religious authority from the priesthood and return it to the monarchy, a king by the name of Amenhotep revolted. Amenhotep denied the existence of Amen-Ra and all other gods. According to him, the only true god was Aten, the sun disk, and Amenhotep was Aten's high priest. Amenhotep renamed himself Akhenaten ("servant of Aten"). He closed all the temples and constructed a new capital around his solar monotheism. Not only the priests but the people at large were scandalized This was called "The New Kingdom." Bolstered by a strong military and a feeling of religious patriotism, the Egyptians of the New Kingdom successfully repelled an invasion of the Sea Peoples. The Sea Peoples were a mysterious race of marauders who had managed to destabilize other parts of the Mediterranean. The New Kingdom finally abandoned the practice of pyramid building. Instead they buried kings in rock-cut tombs. It was in such a tomb where the famous mummified body of Tutankhamun was discovered. Tutankhamun was important because his mummy is perhaps the most famous example of Egyptian life and burial practices extant today.

CLEOPATRA

Assignment

Why did Cleopatra get involved in the Roman Civil War (after the assassination of Julius Caesar)?

Answer: Cleopatra was the consummate Egyptian patriot and saw this as a way to advance the cause of her nation. During July of the year 46 BC, Caesar returned to Rome. He was given many honors and a ten-year dictatorship. These celebrations lasted from September to October and he brought Cleopatra over, along with her entourage. The conservative Republicans were extremely offended when he established Cleopatra in his home. During the time that followed, Cleopatra watched carefully to see who would be the next power in Rome. She was invited by Mark Antony to Tarsus in 41 BC. Cleopatra and Antony spent the winter of 41–40 in Alexandria. In the spring of 40 BC, Mark Antony left Cleopatra and returned home. He did not see her for four years. When he returned he married Cleopatra. Meanwhile, Octavia, Antony's divorced wife, attacked Antony. Octavian's navy severely defeated Antony in Actium, Greece, on September 2, 31 BC. Octavian's admiral, Agrippa, planned and carried out the defeat. In less than a year, Antony half-heartedly defended Alexandria against the advancing army of Octavian. After the defeat, Antony committed suicide by falling on his own sword in 30 BC. After Antony's death, Cleopatra was taken to Octavian where her role in Octavian's triumph was carefully explained to her. He had no interest in any relationship, negotiation, or reconciliation with the queen of Egypt. She would be displayed as a slave in the cities she had ruled over. She decided she would not live that way, so she had an asp, which was an Egyptian cobra, brought to her hidden in a basket of figs. She died on August 12, 30 BC, at the age of 39. The Egyptian religion declared that death by snakebite would secure immortality. With this, she achieved her dying wish, not to be forgotten.

EXAM KEY

Timeline (25 points)

Number these events in the right order.

3   A.   Moses led the Hebrews from exile.

2   B.   Amon-Ra was the primary god.

5   C.   Cleopatra was queen.

4   D.   Alexander the Great conquered Egypt.

1   E.   Pyramids were first built.

Timeline (75 points)

Discuss the most enduring legacy of Egyptian history.

Answer: Historian Chris Freeman in his book *The Legacy of Ancient Egypt* states, "To its neighbors, Egypt was a land of 'gold as plentiful as dust'—a kingdom to be admired and envied, but too powerful to be taken. Other kingdoms rose and fell; Egypt endured. To the early Greeks—who arrived late in Egypt's long history - it was the home of an almost unimaginably ancient written language and equally ancient, mysterious religious traditions that were rumored to hold the secrets of the gods. To the Romans, Egypt was the granary that fed their empire, and a source of strange gods and exotic objects that fascinated everyone from slave to emperor. Only the Arabs, who arrived nearly 1,000 years after the fall of the last Egyptian dynasty, found a nearly clean slate on which to inscribe their history with little reference to the old. Over the course of the last 400 years, our picture of the land of the pharaohs has been built up piece by piece, leaving plenty of gaps for the imagination to fill in. Paradoxically, in the 20th century—when most of Egypt's past has finally been well documented—the more familiar and everyday it becomes, the more there is a desire to cling to the exotic, the mysterious, the impenetrable. The Egypt of the imagination, which has had a hold on Western culture since its origins in classical Greece—a hold that shows no sign of diminishing—is perhaps the most enduring quality of Egypt."

Chapter 5

EGYPTIAN LIFE

First Thoughts . . .

From the beginning, the Egyptian religion, lifestyle, and world view developed from living in proximity of the mighty Nile River. Communities of hunter-gatherers made the Nile River the center of community life. The drying up of the Sahara increasingly confined them to the river area. No problem. Soon these communities became sufficiently stable to be united in a single political entity. Egyptian culture was born.

Chapter Learning Objectives . . .

As a result of this chapter you should be able to:

1. Speculate on the dangers of individualism to a Christian walk.
   Answer Question 1-A

2. React to Pyrrho's belief that "things are equally indifferent, immeasurable, and inarbitrable."
   Answer Question 1-B

3. Contrast the Egyptian views of the afterlife with Christian views of the afterlife.
   Answer Assignment 2

4. Describe life in an ancient Egyptian family.
   Answer Assignment 3

5. List the attributes of God that were manifested in His deliverance of the Israelites from Egypt.
   Answer Assignment 4

6. Contrast the God of Jews and Christians with the Egyptian god Amon-Ra.
   Answer Chapter Exam

LESSON 1

PHILOSOPHERS AND WORLD VIEWS

Assignment

A. Individualism—a by-product of Cynicism—was the watchword for the self-indulgent 1960s. What are the dangers of individualism (or privatism) to a Christian walk?

Answer: Central to Christian maturation is submission to authority and participation in a family (i.e., the Church). The challenge to Christians is to have a significant relationship with God—through the spiritual disciplines—and to have significant relationships with brothers and sisters in Christ. Our calling is to represent the One who has redeemed us, making both our God and His kingdom known. Faith is meaningless without works, but works are hollow without the manifest presence of God. While Christians are saved by grace through faith, and it is a very personal event, subsequently they are called to work together in the Body of Christ to advance the Kingdom of God.

B. React to Pyrrho's idea that "things are equally indifferent, unmeasurable, and inarbitrable."

Answer: This is a mindless assessment of a world without God. Of course God is alive and present and very much involved in human affairs. Thus everything has meaning and importance. Cynicism is another form of agnosticism, or disbelief. Christians should not participate in such a world view.

LESSON 2

EGYPTIAN RELIGION

Assignment

Contrast the Egyptian views of the afterlife with Christian views of the afterlife.

Answer: In Egyptian religions, the deceased went to a place with whatever possessions he could carry. The status of the person in life was more important, therefore, than his behavior. His belief system was incidental. Ancient Egyptian civilization was based on religion; their belief in the rebirth after death became the driving force behind their funeral practices. Death was simply a temporary interruption, rather than complete cessation, of life, and eternal life could be ensured by means of preservation of the physical form through mummification and the provision of statuary and other funerary equipment. Each human consisted of the physical body, the "ka", the "ba", and the "akh." The Name and Shadow were also living entities. To enjoy the afterlife, all these elements had to be sustained and protected from harm. In Christianity everyone has an eternal existence— the question is where will eternity be spent? With God? Or separated from God? The former is an undeserved, free gift from God but requires the believer to make a personal, public confession of faith in Jesus Christ, God's Son who died to pay the penalty of sin that would separate us from God's presence.

EGYPTIAN PEOPLE

Assignment

Describe what your life would be like if you lived in an average ancient Egyptian family.

Answer: The life of an ancient Egyptian was short and difficult. Newborn children were not likely to survive their first year. The infant mortality rate was extremely high, possibly around 60–70 percent, and the mortality rate for women in childbirth was also extremely high. Many, if not most, Egyptian women died in childbirth before their 30th birthday. Children then were seen as a special blessing from the gods if they survived their first year. At approximately age five, boys and girls were separated in their learning experiences. Boys from wealthy families went to school. Boys from poor families began helping with the men's jobs in the fields or whatever other occupations their fathers happened to hold (e.g., carpenter). A boy's education lasted until he was between 12 and 16, at which time he was considered to be an adult who could begin to work for himself. The earliest age for men to marry was 16, but normally they were between 17 and 20 years of age when they took their first wife. Men could have several wives, but, in fact, very few did. It was too expensive to have more than one wife. As a result, this was usually done only by the very wealthy. Most men continued to work until they died. No one retired. The average life span was approximately 30 years of age for a poor working man, 25 for a poor woman. Making it past the age of 40 was rare. Girls' lives were much different from boys'. Girls' lives were centered in the home and the family. At age four, girls would begin to learn from their mothers how to maintain a household. They learned how to sew, prepare food, and keep house. The hours spent doing domestic chores were much longer than the educational hours of boys. Cloth had to be woven and then sewn into clothing, the fields planted and tended, food prepared, and countless other household chores performed. Girls were expected to marry at about age 12 or 13, although there is evidence of girls marrying as young as 8 or 9 years of age. Widows were to be taken care of by their sons. If a women had no sons she was to be taken care of by her daughter and son-in-law, but this was rare and occurred only if the daughter had become part of a wealthier family. It was more likely that widows would be forced to live as beggars.

EGYPT AND THE HEBREWS

Assignment

List the attributes of the Hebrews' God manifested in His deliverance of His people from Egypt.

Answer: God is an awesome God. He controls all human governments and even nature itself. He is a just God. He will not tolerate injustice forever. He is in covenant with His chosen people. He will honor His agreements. He loves humankind for no other reason than He chose to do so. God controls all human governments and even nature itself. In delivering His people, the Egyptian Pharaoh released the Hebrews and God made a path for them through the Red Sea.

Discussion Question: 150–200 Words (100 points)

Compare and contrast the following passages quoted from the Egyptian and Hebrew writings.

The following is a quote from an Egyptian text honoring the god Amon-Ra:

Behold, the Osiris Ani, the scribe of the holy offerings of all the gods, saith: Homage to thee, O thou who hast come as Khepera, Khepera the creator of the gods, Thou art seated on thy throne, thou risest up in the sky, illumining thy mother [Nut], thou art seated on thy throne as the king of the gods. [Thy] mother Nut stretcheth out her hands, and performeth an act of homage to thee. The domain of Manu receiveth thee with satisfaction. The goddess Maat embraceth thee at the two seasons of the day. May Ra give glory, and power, and truth-speaking, and the appearance as a living soul so that he may gaze upon Heru-khuti, to the KA of the Osiris the Scribe Ani, who speaketh truth before Osiris, and who saith: Hail, O all ye gods of the House of the Soul, who weigh heaven and earth in a balance, and who give celestial food [to the dead]. Hail, Tatun, [who art] One, thou creator of mortals [and] of the Companies of the Gods of the South and of the North, of the West and of the East, ascribe ye praise to Ra, the lord of heaven, the KING, Life, Strength, and Health, the maker of the gods.

The following passage is Psalm 89:1-18:

I will sing of the LORD's great love forever; with my mouth I will make your faithfulness known through all generations. I will declare that your love stands firm forever, that you have established, your faithfulness in heaven itself.

You said, "I have made a covenant with my chosen one, I have sworn to David my servant, 'I will establish your line forever and make your throne firm through all generations.'" Selah

The heavens praise your wonders, O LORD , your faithfulness too, in the assembly of the holy ones. For who in the skies above can compare with the Lord? Who is like the LORD among the heavenly beings? In the council of the holy ones God is greatly feared; he is more awesome than all who surround him. Who is like you, LORD God Almighty? You, LORD, are mighty, and your faithfulness surrounds you.

You rule over the surging sea; when its waves mount up, you still them. You crushed Rahab like one of the slain; with your strong arm you scattered your enemies. The heavens are yours, and yours also the earth; you founded the world and all that is in it. You created the north and the south; Tabor and Hermon sing for joy at your name. Your arm is endued with power; your hand is strong, your right hand exalted.

Righteousness and justice are the foundation of your throne; love and faithfulness go before you. Blessed are those who have learned to acclaim you, who walk in the light of your presence, LORD. They rejoice in your name all day long; they celebrate your righteousness. For you are their glory and strength, and by your favor you exalt our horn. Indeed, our shield belongs to the LORD, our king to the Holy One of Israel.

Answer: The Egyptian passage clearly does show adoration and reverence for the god Ra. The author is exuberant in his metaphors, enthusiastic in his sincerity. Ra is omniscient—he controls everything. But David, in his psalm, not only presents an omnipotent God. His God loves David, and David loves his God! The notion that God loves his creation so much, to be personally involved with that Creation, is a notion completely alien to Egyptian theology.

Chapter 6

GREECE

First Thoughts . . .

The great Greek historian Edith Hamilton, speaking about Greece, said, "Civilization . . . is a matter of imponderables, of delight in the things of the mind, of love of beauty, of honor, grace, courtesy, delicate feeling. Where imponderables are things of first importance, there is the height of civilization, and if, at the same time, the power of art exists unimpaired, human life has reached a level seldom attained and very seldom surpassed." To Hamilton, to all mankind, Greece was the height of imponderables. What was then produced of art and thought has never been surpassed and very rarely equaled, and its stamp is still evident on all the art and all the thought of the Western world.

Chapter Learning Objectives . . .

As a result of this chapter you should be able to:

1. Give examples of how the mountainous terrain of the Greek Peninsula affected the way Greek civilization evolved.
   Answer Assignment 1

2. Explain why the city-states emerged as the main political entities in Greece.
   Answer Assignment 2

3. Evaluate where you would rather live: ancient Athens or Sparta.
   Answer Assignment 3

4. Pretend that you are offering to guide a future traveler through your town or city or rural area.
   Answer Assignment 4

5. In light of your understanding of Greek culture and history, interpret 1 Corinthians 15.
   Answer Chapter Exam

LESSON 1

GRECIAN HISTORY

Assignment

Give examples of how the mountainous terrain of the Greek Peninsula affected the way Greek civilization evolved.

Answer: Never has a civilization been so influenced by its geography. The mountains, which served as natural barriers and boundaries, dictated the political and economic character of Greece. Agriculture was possible, even desirable in limited, isolated pockets, but there was no room for vast wheat or barley fields such as those of Egypt's delta. Therefore, the Greek economy, from its genesis, was diversified and interdependent. The geography also dictated that the Greeks live in independent, isolated communities. Eventually these communities were organized into city-states. The inhospitable landscape obligated the Greeks to look beyond their borders to the sea and to their adjoining Mediterranean communities to subsidize the paltry agrarian options open to them. Geography also encouraged the Greek people to be vigorous and intuitive, even whimsical—characteristics reflected in their gods. The Greeks introduced the idea that the universe was orderly, that man's senses were valid and, as a consequence, that man's proper purpose was to live his own life to the fullest. Egyptian gods were partly anthropomorphic; Greek gods were supermen.

LESSON 2

GROWTH OF GREEK CIVILIZATION

Assignment

Why did the city-states emerge as the main political entities in Greece?

Answer: Isolated villages started to band together to form strong trading centers. These groups of villages that banded together were called city-states. Soon, hundreds of city-states had formed in ancient Greece. The ancient Greeks referred to themselves as citizens of their individual city-states. Each city-state (polis) had its own personality, goals, laws, and customs. Ancient Greeks were very loyal to their city-state. The city-states had many things in common. They all believed in the same gods. They all spoke the same language. But if you asked an ancient Greek where he was from, he would not say, "I live in Greece." If he was from Sparta, he would say, "I am a Spartan." If he lived in Athens, he would say, "I am Athenian." The city-states might band together to fight a common foe. They also went to war with each other. Greece was not yet one country. Ancient Greece was a collection of Greek city-states.

LESSON 3

SPARTA

Assignment

Would you rather live in ancient Athens or Sparta? Why?

Answer: Answers will vary. Athens was a democracy and a Mecca for the arts. This reader, therefore, would prefer to live in Athens. Sparta was a militaristic culture and celebrated noble human characteristics, but this reader would prefer the peace and prosperity of Athens.

A DAY IN OLD ATHENS: A SPECULATIVE ESSAY

Assignment

Pretend that you are offering to guide a future traveler through your town or city or rural area. What would you highlight?

Answer: Answers will vary. Presumably the student would show his visitors the library, his church, the post office, etc. He would choose buildings and locations that were important to him. He would also highlight locations that were important to his society and culture.

Questions: 60-100 Words (50 points each)

A. Professor Anne Mahoney asks, "Always to be the best and be pre-eminent among the others': this is the heroic code as stated by characters in Homer's *Iliad*. What kind of society is built on such a code? Is this ideal compatible with a participatory democracy, in which every citizen has a voice and a vote? Is there a place for heroes in the world of the city?" Answer her question.

Answer: While egalitarian societies (i.e., democratic societies) invite a certain leveling effect, where everyone is equal, that does not mean a democracy does not need and should not have heroes. Christian youth leader Ray Cotton writes: "We all want to look up to someone, somebody who models a lifestyle we admire. These people need not be perfect—we know that perfect people only exist in the comic books—but they should be individuals who have risen above the circumstances of life to accomplish something significant. And, we want our heroes to be above self-promotion and climbing on the backs of others. But this is where the problem lies. In today's world of widespread self-centeredness, it is very difficult to find those heroes from whom we can gain a right perspective of the world about us. Did I say that only comic book heroes are perfect? Even the comic characters are more flawed than we may want to admit. The comic books of today hardly resemble the comic books of the past. Today's comics are often full of violence, sexual themes, and grotesque imagery."

B. Greeks were a fierce warrior people who loved their art and their democracy. As one historian explains, "To the Greeks, what was beautiful was holy; to the Jews, what was holy was beautiful. These views were bound to clash." We see that tension reflected in the apostle Paul's letter to the Corinthians. Read 1 Corinthians 15, and in light of the above quote, and your understanding of Greek culture and history, write an interpretive summary of this biblical chapter.

Answer: Paul is speaking to a people who value the present, who do not understand, or grasp, the importance of the eternal. To the Greek, there is no heaven. All languish is one level of Hades. Therefore the present is most important. Matthew Henry in his commentary states, "In this chapter the apostle treats of that great article of Christianity—the resurrection of the dead.

I. He establishes the certainty of our Savior's resurrection (v. 1–11).

II. He, from this truth, sets himself to refute those who said there is no resurrection of the dead (v. 12–19).

III. From our Savior's resurrection he establishes the resurrection of the dead and confirms the Corinthians in the belief of it by some other considerations (v. 20–34).

IV. He answers an objection against this truth, and takes occasion thence to show what a vast change will be made in the bodies of believers at the resurrection (v. 35–50).

V. He informs us what a change will be made in those who shall be living at the sound of the last trumpet, and the complete conquest the just shall then obtain over death and the grave (v. 51–57).

VI. He sums up the argument with a very serious exhortation to Christians, to be resolved and diligent in their Lord's service, because they know they shall be so gloriously rewarded by him (v. 58)."

Chapter 7

LIFE IN ATHENS: PART ONE

First Thoughts . . .

Historian William Stearns Davis writes, "To three ancient nations the men of the 20th century owe an incalculable debt. To the Jews we owe most of our notions of religion; to the Romans we owe traditions and examples in law, administration, and the general management of human affairs which still keep their influence and value; and finally, to the Greeks we owe nearly all our ideas as to the fundamentals of art, literature, and philosophy, in fact, of almost the whole of our intellectual life." These Greeks lived in many city-states, with Sparta and Athens being central. Sparta was a great military nation most famous for its warrior prowess, but it created not a single great poet, and certainly never a philosopher or sculptor. The civilized life of Greece, during the centuries when she was accomplishing the most, was peculiarly located in Athens. Sophocles, Plato, and Herodotus developed their genius in Athens. They were the ripe products of a society that, in its excellences and weaknesses, presented some of the most interesting pictures and examples in the world. However, to understand the Athenian civilization and genius, it is not enough to know its wars, laws, and politicians. In this chapter we will see Athens as an average Athenian saw it and lived in it from day to day.

Chapter Learning Objectives . . .

As a result of this chapter you should be able to:

1. Discuss what life was like for Greek women.
   Answer Assignment 1

2. Analyze why infanticide was practiced by some Greek families.
   Answer Assignment 2

3. Speculate why slavery was tolerated and even encouraged.
   Answer Assignment 3

4. Discuss Athenian family life and education.
   Answer Assignment 4

5. Describe a typical Athenian citizen.
   Answer Chapter Exam

ATHENIAN WOMEN

Assignment

Greek women could not vote, did not own property, and, generally speaking, did not have any rights at all. Yet, in the Athenian democracy, they seemed, by and large, to be very contented with their station in life. Why?

Answer: As William Stearns Davis in *A Day in Old Athens* (1914) explains:

Assuredly the Athenian house mother cannot match her husband in discussing philosophy or foreign politics, but she has her own home problems and confronts them well. A dozen or twenty servants must be kept busy. From her, all the young children must get their first education and the girls probably everything they are taught until they are married. Even if she does not meet many men, she will strive valiantly to keep the good opinion of her husband. Her husband has turned over to her the entire management of the household. This means that if he is

an easy-going man, she soon understands his home business far better than he does himself, and really has him quite at her mercy. Between caring for her husband's wants, nursing the sick slaves, acting as arbitress in their inevitable disputes, keeping a constant watch upon the storeroom, and finally in attending to the manufacture of nearly all the family clothing, she is not likely to rust in busy idleness, or sit complaining of her lot. At the many great public festivals she is always at least an onlooker and often she marches proudly in the magnificent processions. She is allowed to attend the tragedies in the theater. Probably, too, the family will own a country farm, and spend a part of the year thereon. Here she will be allowed a delightful freedom of movement, impossible in the closely built city. All in all, then, she will complain of too much enforced activity rather than of too much idleness.

FAMILY LIFE

Assignment

Why do you think some fathers purposely murdered their newborn children?

Answer: To notify the neighbors of a birth of a child, a woolen strip was hung over the front door—this indicated a female baby. An olive branch indicated a boy had been born. Families did not always keep their new child. After a woman had a baby, she would show it to her husband. If the husband accepted it, it would live, but if he refused it, it would die. Babies would often be rejected if they were illegitimate, unhealthy, or deformed, the

wrong sex (female for example), or too great a burden on the family. These babies would not be directly killed, but put in a clay pot or jar and deserted outside the front door or on the roadway. In ancient Greek religion, this practice took the responsibility away from the parents because the child would die of natural causes, for example hunger, asphyxiation, or exposure to the elements. If the baby were accepted, there would be a celebration: he or she would be given a name and presented to the gods and goddesses.

SLAVERY IN ATHENS

Assignment

In a democracy such as Athens, why was slavery tolerated or even encouraged?

Answer: In fact, there is not one—not one!—anti-slavery pamphlet, essay, or poem written. Neither Plato nor Aristotle discussed the issue. In fact, they, and

other philosophers, ignored slavery altogether. Apparently, they thought it was an appropriate, moral, ethical institution. Certainly, most contemporaries thought it was critical to the maintenance of Greek life as they knew it.

LESSON 4

EDUCATION
Assignment

Athenian education emphasized moral education. Students were taught to read and to write, but they were also taught principles of good citizenship. Given the present state of education in America's public schools, explain the dangers of separating the values of society from its educational system.

Answer: Public schools are poor socialization agents. They were not designed to teach morality, for that best occurs in the home and in church. With both institutions under great stress, no wonder public education is not working.

EXAM KEY

Essay Question: 100-150 Words (100 points)

Write a short essay describing a typical Athenian citizen. Discuss family life and education. Contrast the lives of free persons with lives of slaves, and lives of women with lives of men.

Answer: Athens in the fifth and sixth century BC was divided into three distinct groups: the citizens, the metics, and the slaves. The citizens, who numbered at the most about 160,000, included only those born of citizen parents, except for the few who were occasionally enfranchised by special law. The metics, who probably did not exceed a total of 100,000, were resident aliens, chiefly non-Athenian Greeks, although some were Phoenicians and Jews. Save for the fact that they had no political privileges and generally were not permitted to own land, the metics had equal opportunities with citizens. They could engage in any occupation they desired and participate in any social or intellectual activities. Slaves were very well treated and were often rewarded for faithful service by being set free. They could work for wages and own property, and some of them held responsible positions as minor public officials and as managers of banks. Life in Athens stands out in rather sharp contrast to that in most other civilizations. One of its leading features was the amazing degree of social and economic equality which prevailed among all the inhabitants. Although there were many who were poor, there were few who were very rich. The average wage was the same for practically all classes of workers, skilled and unskilled alike. Nearly everyone, whether citizen, metic, or slave, ate the same kind of food, wore the same kind of clothing, and participated in the same kind of amusement. This substantial equality was enforced in part by the system of liturgies, which were services to the state rendered by wealthy men, chiefly in the form of contributions to support the drama, equip the navy, or provide for the poor.

A second outstanding characteristic of Athenian life was its poverty in comforts and luxuries. Part of this was due to the low income of the mass of the people. Teachers, sculptors, masons, carpenters, and common laborers all received the same standard wage of one drachma (about 30 cents) per day. Part of it may have been due also to the mild climate, which made possible a life of simplicity. But whatever the cause, the fact remains that, in comparison with modern standards, the Athenians endured an exceedingly impoverished existence. They knew nothing of such common things as watches, soap, newspapers, cotton cloth, sugar, tea, or coffee. Their beds had no springs, their houses had no drains, and their food consisted chiefly of barley cakes, onions, and fish, washed down with diluted wine. From the standpoint of clothing they were no better off. A rectangular piece of cloth wrapped around the body and fastened with pins at the shoulders and with a rope around the waist served as the main garment. A larger piece was draped around the body as an extra garment for outdoor wear. No one wore either stockings or socks, and few had any footgear except sandals (www.greek-thesaurus.gr).

LIFE IN ATHENS: PART TWO

First Thoughts . . .

Greece is a country surrounded by water, so the sea has always played an important role in its economy, particularly in Athens. Enterprising Athenians were skillful seafarers who tapped into existing markets and created new ones at coastal sites across the Mediterranean Sea. By the seventh and sixth centuries BC, Greek colonies and settlements stretched all the way from western Asia Minor to southern Italy, Sicily, North Africa, and even to the coasts of southern France and Spain. Science, especially in the area of medicine, assured the success of these commercial enterprises. Likewise, the Greek army and navy, the most formidable of their era, assured the safety and continued success of Athenian citizens and businessmen.

Chapter Learning Objectives . . .

As a result of this chapter you should be able to:

1. Discuss why Greek religion and medicine were naturally connected.
   Answer Question 1-A

2. Speculate as to why such a connection seems comparatively absent from American medicine.
   Answer Question 1-B

3. Compare ancient Athenian business to contemporary business.
   Answer Assignment 2

4. Explain why Greek armies were so successful.
   Answer Assignment 3

5. Explain what a "trireme" was and why it was such an effective instrument of warfare.
   Answer Assignment 4

6. Evaluate why a peace-loving Athenian democracy was so skillful in conducting warfare.
   Answer Assignment 5

LESSON 1

MEDICINE

Assignment

Why, in Greek thought, were religion and medicine naturally connected? Why do you think such a connection is not as greatly respected in American medicine?

Answer: The healing arts were not separated from religion. Certain gods were devoted to the healing arts, and the temple was also the hospital. A patient slept overnight in the temple, and the gods in theory visited him in a dream, revealing a course of treatment that would lead to recovery. No doubt there was a lot of chicanery involved, and surely many patients did not get better. However, there are documented cases of many being healed, perhaps due to the hope they received or to a positive attitude. The value of mental therapeutics was, and still is, recognized as beneficial to healing. However, not all medicine was left to the priests and the gods. Attached to the temple were skilled physicians who "interpreted" a patient's dream and offered opportunities for prolonged residence with treatment by baths, purgation, dieting, mineral waters, sea baths, all kinds of mild gymnastics, etc. "Suffice it to say, the sonorous connection of religion and science was abundantly evident in the medicinal interventions available in Athens." Post-Enlightenment Europe and America have more or less decided to keep medicine separate from religion.

LESSON 2

BUSINESS AND TRADE

Assignment

In Greece, a vocation in business was perceived as inferior to one in the arts. In America, big business seems to control everything—art, business, health care, and even religion. Why?

Answer: In Greek society the arts and education were esteemed a great deal more than business. In America, business controls almost everything—education, health care, even the arts. This is not to denigrate business, but it is to say, in an obviously capitalistic society like America, business is far more important than it was in Athenian society.

LESSON 3

THE ATHENIAN ARMY

Assignment

Why were Greek armies so successful?

Answer: The organization of the Athenian army was brilliant in its simplicity; each of the ten Athenian tribes sent its own special battalion. A unit of the Athenian citizen army, like practically all Greek armies, was comprised of heavily armed infantry soldiers—the hoplites. Hoplites had javelins, and sometimes slings and bows. They carried small but deadly swords. They were the heart of the Athenian army and the reason it was so successful. The use of hoplites was an ingenious way to have an effective fighting force without maintaining a standing army. Tactics were simple and easily learned. Hoplites usually fought in the deadly and highly effective phalanx. Hoplites formed long, parallel lines, close to each other. Every hoplite carried a large, round shield that covered his own left side and the right side of the man to his left. A phalanx was, therefore, very densely packed and could not easily turn to the left or the right. It was highly effective and guaranteed Greek military victory for a century and a half. The Greeks had neither flags nor standards, and gave no medals for valor. There were no division signs or emblems. Every citizen was expected to do his duty with valor and ingenuity. The notion that one soldier was isolated from all others for recognition was not considered. What was fundamental Greek strategy? First, Greek generals selected a broad stretch of level ground for the struggle, since stony, hilly, or uneven ground would never do for the maneuvering of hoplites. The two opposing armies exchanged derisive shouts and catcalls. Almost never did fighting occur at night. When the general was ready, the phalanx advanced on the run. At first the phalanx pushed into the middle of the enemy. In fact, it appeared that the Greeks would surely be destroyed. Then, from within the phalanx emerged fierce Greek swordsmen. This Greek killing machine descended on their enemies like a mighty storm. At battle's end, huge numbers of enemy casualties would clutter the ground. A Greek army could defeat a foe 100 times its size. The Phalanx would continue to advance, enlarge, and move like a massive, deadly reaper across the field.

LESSON 4
THE ATHENIAN NAVY

Assignment

What was the trireme and why was it such an effective instrument of warfare?

Answer: Triremes were ships built for speed and mobility; however, they were killing machines. They were 120 feet long and were powered by 170 rowers. They were built low to the ground, so the lowest lines of rowers were just 18 inches above the waterline. The ships were quite narrow, which meant that they were not built to handle the open ocean. Battles therefore occurred close to shore or in narrow straits. Most of the crew officers were Athenian citizens. The rowers were not slaves, as many assume, but were paid rowers. Besides the rowers, a trireme's crew included 14 spearmen and 4 archers. These were the "marines" of the Greek navy.

EXAM KEY

Essay Question: 100-150 Words (100 points)

Why was the ancient peace-loving, democratic Athenian society so skillful at conducting warfare?

Answer: The ingenious, peace-loving, democratic Athenian army was second to none (except the Spartan army). Ancient Greeks invented the use of technology in warfare. It was the base of military superiority of the civilization of the West. The first such invention was the Phalanx, which devastated all enemies. The Athenians produced very fast triremes. The Greeks in Sicily developed the first advanced catapults. The citizen soldier, in fact, coupled with advanced technology, made the Greek army unbeatable.

Chapter 9

GREEK WARS

First Thoughts . . .

In ancient Greece, a new system of warfare evolved; weaponry, tactics, ideas and formations changed. Modified by Philip II and mainly by Alexander the Great after the Macedonians conquered Greece, this new age of warfare lasted until the rise of the Roman Empire, when the legion formation became the general method of battle. Ironically, this new battle system ultimately caused the demise of the Greek military, because it resulted in Greeks conquering other Greeks during the Peloponnesian War. Yet nothing could quell Greek culture—Alexander the Great made sure of that.

Chapter Learning Objectives . . .

As a result of this chapter you should be able to:

1. Contrast Greek religion and ethics with those of Hebrew contemporaries in Palestine.
   Answer Assignment 1

2. Evaluate why the Greeks won the Persian Wars.
   Answer Assignment 2

3. Evaluate why the Spartans won the Peloponnesian War.
   Answer Assignment 3

4. Pretend that you live in AD 55 Athens, and share the gospel with a potential Greek convert.
   Answer Chapter Exam Question A

5. Discuss what legacy Alexander the Great left to the world.
   Answer Assignment 4, Chapter Exam Question B

Assignment

The Greeks kept their formal religion (but not their morality) separate from their daily lives. They relied on their religion for cultic rituals and religious superstitions, but for issues concerning everyday life, they consulted oracles and philosophers. Contrast the Greek way of life with that of their Hebrew contemporaries in Palestine.

Answer: Greek religion was a typical form of early paganism, which means it was polytheistic, consisting of the worship of many gods. The gods had a job to do. The Greeks believed that the gods would offer protection and guide their city-states. This was the same expectation shared by other ancient civilizations. Greeks believed that they had to worship and please the gods to have good fortune, so they participated in ceremonies and sacrifices in order to curry the favor of their gods. To that end, temples were erected as places to offer sacrifices to the gods. The Greeks also firmly believed that this life was not the only reality in which the soul lives, but after this lifetime, a whole new and different one awaited them. Adherents didn't believe in personal salvation, per se, which no doubt troubled many of them, but their Greek traditions required that they live a humble life in proper abeyance to their gods and goddesses. Greek religion made no claims of universality, so its people did not try to convert others. They had no priests, sacred texts, or moral code (e.g., Hammurabi Code; Ten Commandments) backed by religious beliefs. Greek religion was essentially a body of myths designed to explain natural phenomena and to highlight desirable character traits that good Greek citizens were expected to exhibit. Each city-state had its favorite gods and goddesses, a tradition that cemented the body of citizens into a loyal community. The gods and goddesses, however, were more like modern college mascots than omniscient deities.

Assignment

In spite of the fact that the Persians substantively outnumbered the Greeks, the Greeks won the Persian Wars. Why?

Answer: Time and time again, Greek ingenuity, technology, and battle tactics enabled them to defeat the frustrated Persians. While King Leonidas and his 300 Spartans delayed the Persians at Thermopylae, Themistocles and his Greek navy waited. Finally, the Greeks met the Persians off the island of Salamis. The Athenians destroyed most of the Persian fleet. The Persian army retreated. It is difficult to assess all the consequences of the Greek victory over the Persians. While the Spartans were principally responsible for the land victory, the Athenian fleet was probably the most important component of that victory. The alliances that Athens would make following the retreat of the Persians, the so-called Delian League, made Athens the premier Greek city-state. This power would make Athens the cultural center of the Greek world, but it would also make the Spartans increasingly suspicious of Athenian intentions.

LESSON 3

PELOPONNESIAN WARS

Assignment

Why did the Spartans ultimately win the Peloponnesian War?

Answer: Athenian military blunders, a plague, and Spartan military prowess ultimately gave victory to the Spartans. Athens was devastated by a plague imported from Egypt. In fact, Pericles himself died. Athens offered a peace treaty in 430, but Sparta refused. Then, the tables turned again. Athens won several sea battles and it looked as though Sparta would lose after all. This was an unprecedented disgrace for Sparta. This time Sparta sued for peace, which Athens foolishly refused. In 424 BC, all Athenian offensive plans failed. Athenian hopes now rested on taking up an even more bold offensive to cut Spartan and Corinthian supplies from Sicily. In 416 BC, the campaign at first gained momentum. Syracuse was under siege on land and at sea, but Athenian attempts to take the city were thwarted. The Athenian fleet was blocked at the harbor and then defeated in battle. Sparta now had a strong fleet, with additional reinforcements from the west. Athens had lost its best sailors and had nearly exhausted its treasury. With the grain supply from Sicily and from Egypt completely under Spartan control (with some help from Persia), Athens was totally dependent on food from Crimea through the Hellespont. There the Athenian commanders Thrasybulus and Thrasylus defeated the Spartan Mindarus at Cynossema in September of 411 BC. Once more, Sparta requested peace, but Athenian leadership refused again. In autumn of 408 BC, the Spartan navy closed the last avenue of Athenian grain supply. After six months of starvation and no prospect for relief, Athens surrendered on generous terms offered by Sparta. Athens' city walls and those connecting Athens to Piraeus were torn down and the empire dissolved.

LESSON 4

ALEXANDER THE GREAT

Assignment

When others had failed, why was Alexander so successful?

Answer: Alexander the Great, the king of Macedonia and conqueror of the known world, was one of the greatest military geniuses of all times. In control of the entire eastern Mediterranean coast, in 331 BC, Alexander defeated King Darius in a decisive battle. Next, Alexander conquered Babylon itself, and the great Persian Empire was finished. By 326 BC, he reached India, where he stopped. In short, Alexander conquered the entire known world. He fell ill at Babylon and died at age 33. He was buried in Alexandria, Egypt.

Questions: 60-100 Words (50 points each)

A. Pretend that you live in Athens circa AD 45. You belong to a small house church. You are attempting to explain the gospel to your Greek neighbors. To what Scriptures will you refer in trying to convince your neighbors?

Answer: In 1 Corinthian 15 Paul addresses many of the issues that concerned Greeks: particularly the issue of the resurrection. Also this reader would offer Scripture that invites the Greek hearer to use his mind to see the Light. See Titus 2:11—"For the grace of God that brings salvation has appeared to all men," and 1 Peter 1:10—"Concerning this salvation, the prophets, who spoke of the grace that was to come to you, searched intently and with the greatest care."

B. What legacy did Alexander the Great leave to the world?

Answer: Alexander the Great changed the world in several significant ways. In his astonishing career, Alexander never lost a battle. He was outnumbered a good bit of the time. But, like his Greek predecessors, he won smashing victories over forces superior in numbers. Alexander's success lay in his tactics, particularly the phalanx, which allowed its enemies little openings for attack. More importantly, he understood the importance of cavalry as an offensive weapon. Cavalry could also compensate for a smaller army. He was also adept at changing tactics in the middle of a battle. Known for his anger, he could also be merciful. He treated his soldiers well. His soldiers were inspired by his example and followed him to what was then the ends of the earth. And through it all, he never lost sight of his ultimate purpose: to spread the light of Greece into the darkness of the world. Greek influence became the predominant cultural influence for a thousand years (www.socialstudiesforkids.com).

Chapter 10

PHILOSOPHERS AND WORLD VIEWS

First Thoughts . . .

In a real way, the culture war that is raging across America began thousands of years ago in the writings and thoughts of Greek philosophers. Philosopher Alfred Whitehead noted, "Western philosophy is just a series of footnotes to Plato." Indeed. To a large degree the decision that Burger King® makes in ad campaigns more or less reflects a world view decision that is a derivation of Platonic philosophy. Does one emphasize the "spiritual" value of a Whopper? Or the "sensual" value of a Whopper? These two questions have set the perameters of world view discussion since before Christ was born. How did it begin? Greek philosophers did something no one, other than the Hebrew prophets, had done: They broke away from a mythological approach to explaining the world, and for the first time used reason and evidence to discuss ontology (i.e., the beginning of things). Initially concerned with explaining the entire cosmos, Greek philosophers strived to identify its single underlying principle. This changed the world forever.

Chapter Learning Objectives . . .

As a result of this chapter you should be able to:

1. Analyze Herodotus' teachings.
   Answer Assignment 1

2. Discuss the Ionian philosophers and their connection with modern philosophy.
   Answer Assignment 2

3. Analyze Pythagoras and his philosophy.
   Answer Assignment 3-A, 3-B, 3-C

4. Compare Socrates' views with Christian orthodoxy.
   Answer Assignment 4-A, 4-B, Chapter Exam

5. Evaluate Aristotle's "Golden Mean."
   Answer Assignment 4-C

HISTORY MAKER: HERODOTUS

Assignment

Highlight several biblical references confirmed by Herodotus' teachings.

Answer: Both the Bible and Herodotus refer to Joseph's living in Egypt. The biblical account goes on to describe how the wife of an Egyptian leader, Potiphar, tried to seduce the young Joseph (Gen. 39:7–10). Herodotus tells of an Egyptian ruler who, for the sake of performing an experiment, searched at length for a married woman who had been faithful to her husband. Herodotus mentions that whereas the Egyptian women transported burdens upon their shoulders, the men carried them upon their heads. This is the very opposite of the custom found in other countries. This is described by both Herodotus and the Bible. Finally, when Joseph, who had become second in command throughout Egypt, received his estranged brothers into his house, they were given water with which to wash their feet (Gen. 43:24). Herodotus recorded a story of an Egyptian ruler who had a golden foot-pan in which his guests were provided water to wash their feet. Another example is Herodotus' and the Bible's similar descriptions of the Assyrian king Sennacherib's siege of Jerusalem (2 Kings 18:13ff; Isa. 36:1ff). Ancient Babylon was known as "the jewel of the kingdoms, the glory of the Babylonians' pride" (Isa. 13:19), "the boast of the whole earth" (Jer. 51:41). Herodotus described Babylon in a similar way. Jeremiah alluded to Babylon's massive fortifications (Jer. 51:53, 58).

PRE-SOCRATIC PHILOSOPHY

Assignment

The Ionian philosophers piqued the interest of generations of philosophers and invited later thinkers to merge the visible and invisible worlds without reference to a personal, omniscient God. They were the first philosophers to suggest that material substance explains natural phenomena. It was a mere hop, skip, and jump to the panoply that atheist Carl Sagan developed in the last part of the 20th century. Why?

Answer: Western philosophy grew out of discussions about ultimate things, or things that seemed really important. Those discussions are occurring in different forms today. In the guise of "science," Charles Darwin, and later men like Carl Sagan, speculated upon creation and other ontological things, as if a priori or self-evident, there was no God, much less a God who loved His world so much that He sent His only Begotten Son. This was not even on the Ionian philosophical radar thousands of years ago. Inevitably Ionian philosophy evolved (no pun intended) into a future philosophy/world view (e.g., Carl Sagan) that jeopardized the notion that there was an awesome God.

LESSON 3

SCHOOLS OF THOUGHT
Assignment

A. Phythagoras, as stated earlier, was the first philosopher to require some standard of behavior from his followers. What would a religion be like that did not require any behavioral change in its adherents?

Answer: In fact, most Greek religions were not connected to any moral or ethical code. One merely adored the gods to obtain favor or to appease their wrath. These religions would require relatively little from their adherents and would no doubt engender little commitment too.

B. Discuss how the Theory of Relativity was Eleatic in origin and composition.

Answer: The Eleatic School argued that reality was indivisible and endless. There was no beginning or ending to time, either. All things were the same. From the beginning of time, everything existed that was to exist and that which existed changed in form, but not in substance. Thus, change was impossible. Something might change in form—ice to water to steam—but it was the same in substance. Also, once a thing moved in one direction it continued to move in that direction until time and circumstances stopped it. This is at the heart of the Theory of Relativity. Relativity is a theory of the structure of space and time. It was introduced in Albert Einstein's 1905 paper "On the Electrodynamics of Moving Bodies." Einstein argued:

1. The laws of physics are the same for all observers in uniform motion relative to one another (principle of relativity).

2. The speed of light in a vacuum is the same for all observers, regardless of their relative motion or of the motion of the source of the light.

Furthermore, Einstein argued that two events, simultaneous for one observer, may not be simultaneous for another observer if the observers are in relative motion. Moving clocks are measured to tick more slowly than an observer's "stationary" clock. Objects are measured to be shortened in the direction that they are moving with respect to the observer. $E = mc^2$, energy and mass are equivalent and transmutable. No physical object or message or field line can travel faster than light.

C. Socrates argued that one was not born virtuous, but that he or she could determine to work hard to develop virtue and eventually become virtuous through practice and ongoing open discussion. How is this view contradictory to Christian orthodoxy?

Answer: All have sinned and fallen short of the Kingdom of God! All people are born into original sin and must experience the redemption power of the Cross. Jesus Christ died so that the power of sin could be broken. There simply is no other way that a just God could see imperfect people as virtuous.

PLATO AND ARISTOTLE

Assignment

A. The most famous concept of Plato's work was the concept of love. "Love" to Plato was a "form" from which virtue flowed. Compare and contrast this view of love with a view from a man trained in the teachings of Plato: the apostle Paul.

Answer: To Plato, love is the pursuit of a "form." The notion of "unconditional love," or agape love, is absent from Plato. Love is a yearning to retrieve something that humankind lost when we were "split from each other." Paul, on the other hand, while he agreed that love is something greater than, and separate from, humankind, understood that love is God. It is not merely a "form." Love is personified, manifested, in the love that God has toward His creation. Humankind merely replicates that love one to another.

B. Aristotle said that mankind should strike a balance between passion and temperance, between extremes of all sorts, and that good people should seek the "Golden Mean"—a course of life that is never extreme. What problem does this philosophy present to a Christian believer?

Answer: Desirable ethical behavior is not merely the cessation of human activity. It is not a "balance between passion and temperance." It is turning away from sin, turning away from a walk of selfishness, and inviting Jesus Christ to be Lord of one's life. At the heart of Christian ethics is the Person and Life of Jesus Christ, whose sacrifice on the Cross radically, irrevocably snatched humankind from destruction and gave humans the opportunity to live productive, moral lives. This event was an external act from God, not merely an internal change of human will.

C. Aristotle, for the first time, discussed the gods as if they were quantified entities. He spoke about them as if they were not present. What implications did this have for scientific research?

Answer: Aristotle is the father of empiricism (i.e., the pursuit of knowledge by quantified data), which is the heart of science. There is nothing wrong with empiricism, or rationalism (i.e., logic). However, the really important things in life—love, hope, faith—cannot be quantified or explained empirically. As long as science pursues empiricism with a faithful bent, that is, as long as science recognizes that God is the Creator of all things, science is free to enrich the human knowledge base. However, when science invites people to disbelief, or agnosticism, as the theory of evolution, for instance, has done, then it has gone too far.

EXAM KEY

Map study (30 points)

identify each of the following places by its letter:

C Athens

E Sparta

D Gulf of Corinth

B Peloponnesian Penisula

A Aegean Sea

F Macedonia

Essay Question: 60-100 Words (70 points)

A member of a family is tragically killed in an automobile accident. Discuss how each of the following philosophers would explain this terrible event.

A. Plato

Answer: No problem. The poor person is merely going to Hades, which is not a half bad place. Besides, it is fate. One cannot change one's fate. To the survivor there would be precious little comfort. There is no hope of the Resurrection. There is no hope of spending eternity with a loving God and other loved ones.

B. Aristotle

Answer: Aristotle's answer would be similar to Plato's answer, but he would remind the survivors that death is a physical event and no metaphysical (or other worldly) response can mitigate that the person is dead. Gone.

C. Apostle Paul

Answer: Paul would remind the grieving survivors that Christian believers are more than conquerors in Christ Jesus. While the body will die, the spirit and soul reside somewhere else: heaven or hell. Christian believers live forever with their loving Father in heaven.

Chapter 11

ROMAN HISTORY

First Thoughts . . .

The Romans were the greatest empire builders of the ancient Western world. They created a legacy that is still evident in myriad modern institutions. In many ways, the Roman legacy remains the ideal upon which Western civilization has shaped itself. From a tiny village on the Tiber River to the Euphrates, from the Seine River to Ireland, Roman influence dominated for over 1,000 years. The world has seen nothing like it since and will probably never see anything like it again.

Chapter Learning Objectives . . .

As a result of this chapter you should be able to:

1. Compare the origin of the city-state Rome to the origin of the city-state Athens.
   Answer Assignment 1

2. Evaluate a quote from the historian Edward Gibbon concerning religious freedom.
   Answer Assignment 2

3. Analyze how Christians can prosper in times of persecution.
   Answer Assignment 3

4. Synthesize data and determine why the Roman army was so effective.
   Answer Assignment 5

5. Determine why Rome's success in politics was not matched by its moral integrity.
   Answer Chapter Exam

THE MONARCHY

Assignment

Compare the origin of the city-state Rome with the origin of the city-state Athens.

Answer: Athens emerged as a city-state essentially isolated from foreign opposition. Athens began its history around 4000 or 3000 BC. The Acropolis is a natural defensive position that commands the surrounding plains. The settlement was close enough to the ocean to develop trade but far enough to be safe from foreign nations. Rome, on the other hand, emerged with foreign enemies (i.e., Etruscans) in its midst. After conquering Italy, though, the Italian Peninsula provided the Romans with a secure base from which to expand throughout the Mediterranean and into the European world. Italy was easy to defend and, with its numerous deep-water ports, was an ideal place from which to launch expeditions into the interior Mediterranean world. Italy is a peninsula surrounded on three sides by the sea and protected to the north by part of the Alps mountain range. The climate was generally temperate, although summers are hot in the south. Italy is a peninsula jutting out into the Mediterranean Sea west of Greece. Although Italy does not have mountains covering most of its land as does Greece, ancient Italy was poor in mineral resources. However, the most stunning difference between Italy and Greece was Italy's exponentially larger amount of fertile land. While Greece was poor in fertile land, Italy was wealthy in both land and rainfall, so the two nations developed differently. The Romans began and remained largely an agrarian people. Even in its later stages, Roman culture would identify its values and ideals as agrarian. Italy and Greece were different from each other in other significant ways as well. One was that northern Italy was easily accessible from Europe. The Greeks were protected by a formidable mountain range, whereas the Alps to the north of Italy were not quite as invulnerable. Also, Greece had a warlike Greek population to the north—the Macedonians—to serve as a buffer between themselves and other Europeans. The Romans had no such buffer civilization. As a result, conflict was a fairly constant affair in Italy, so the Romans, along with other peoples on the Italian peninsula, developed a military society fairly early in their history. There was very little time to build temples or to write great literary works.

THE REPUBLIC

Assignment

The historian Edward Gibbon also wrote, "The various modes of worship, which prevailed in the Roman World, were all considered by the people as equally true; by the philosopher as equally false; and by the magistrate as equally useful. And thus toleration produced not only mutual indulgence, but even religious accord." Do you agree/disagree with his assessment?

Answer: S. D. Gaede, in his book *When Tolerance Is No Virtue,* argues that in America there is considerable confusion about toleration, in other words, how Americans ought to live with differences and a cacophony of contradictory justifications for lifestyles opposed to one another. All appeal to the need of tolerance, but there is nothing like common argument on what that means. What is truth? What is toleration? American culture doesn't know the answer to these two questions. But Christians do: Jesus Christ is the Way, the Truth, and the Life. Unfortunately, most Americans have lost confidence in truth and have come to the conclusion that truth is unattainable. Thus, tolerance is an excuse to ignore truth. G. K. Chesterton wrote: "Toleration is the virtue of the man without convictions." The Christian knows what is right and he should do it. Christians affirm truth but recognize relativism for what it is—sin.

THE ROMAN EMPIRE

Assignment

Edward Gibbon, in his masterpiece *Decline and Fall of the Roman Empire*, writes, "Public virtue, which among the ancients was denominated patriotism, is derived from a strong sense of our own interest in the preservation and prosperity of the free government of which we are members. Such a sentiment, which had rendered the legions of the republic almost invincible, could make but a very feeble impression on the mercenary servants of a despotic prince; and it became necessary to supply that defect by other motives, of a different, but not less forcible nature; honor and religion." When pagan religion was replaced by Christianity in AD 400–500, Rome was doomed. Agree or disagree with Gibbon's conclusions.

Answer: This author greatly respects Gibbon, and, in a way, he understands why Gibbon wrote this. However, either Constantine did not truly implement a Christ-centered kingdom (which this author suspects), or Gibbon has it wrong. Christianity has strengthened—not weakened—great political kingdoms. For instance, the Davidic Kingdom was one of the most powerful and successful kingdoms in world history. Likewise, pagan but religious kingdoms in Egypt prospered. The loss of morality, not the advent of Christianity, doomed the Roman Empire.

THE ROMAN MILITARY

Assignment

Why was the Roman army and navy virtually unbeatable for a thousand years?

Answer: Copying some of the strategies of the Greek hoplites, Roman soldiers were an unbeatable force. They regularly beat enemies ten or more times their size. The core of the Roman legion consisted of heavily armored infantry. These soldiers fought in closed ranks. They worked as a team. At every level the men of a legion fought together toward ultimate victory. In contrast, most of the armies Rome faced were comprised of courageous but undisciplined warriors whose personal valor might match that of any individual Roman, but who had no chance against a trained army. This combination of superior organization, esprit de corps, and disciplined armored infantry gave the Romans a tremendous advantage in battle.

Essay Question: 60-100 Words

A. The historian Edward Gibbon wrote, "The various modes of worship, which prevailed in the Roman World, were all considered by the people as equally true; by the philosopher as equally false; and by the magistrate as equally useful. And thus toleration produced not only mutual indulgence, but even religious accord." Why do you agree or disagree with his assessment? Most of us prefer a society that has a high regard for religious freedom and widespread toleration, but what is the danger that this freedom poses? **(75 points)**

Answer: The author wrote the following article for a magazine that captures the essence of this question. It is entitled "The time of Obadiah Is Over."

In 49 BC, the crossing of a small stream in northern Italy by ambitious Roman general Julius Caesar became one of the pivotal events in world history. From it sprang the Roman Empire and the genesis of modern Europe. An ancient Roman law forbade any general from crossing the Rubicon River and entering Italy proper with a standing army. To do so was treason. Caesar was well aware of this. Coming up with his troops on the banks of the Rubicon, he halted, and reminded his fellow officers of the importance of the next step.

"Still we can retreat!" he said. "But once let us pass this little bridge, and nothing is left but to fight it out with arms!" (Suetonius). He crossed the river and we all know the rest.

America is very different from the America in which Karen and I began homeschooling in 1985. Really different. Moral boundaries are violated; sacred fences are down. American in the beginning of the 21st century is spinning out of control. We are stretching our wings adventurously, but drifting farther away from our God. We are in trouble. In 1 Kings 18–19, Elijah and his peers live in a similar world. Choleric Elijah is coming home—and no one wants him to come home. He is crossing his Rubicon. After a long time, in the third year, the word of the LORD came to Elijah: "Go and present yourself to Ahab, and I will send rain on the land." King Ahab and Queen Jezebel, of course, hate him. But even Obadiah, a faithful follower of God and trusted advisor to the king and queen, who had learned so well to survive in this hostile land, who has done so much good for God's people— Obadiah was not too thrilled to see him either. In fact, no one welcomed Elijah—not the hostile king and queen nor the pious evangelical Obadiah.

Even though Elijah brings good news—it is finally going to rain—no one welcomes him. Elijah's fish-or-cut-bait prophetic messages are irritating the life out of the status quo. That is bad enough. But what really scares the dickens out of everyone is the fact that Elijah has come home to Zion, to the City of God, to challenge the gods of the age to a duel.

King Ahab and Jezebel are very capable and, in many ways, successful monarchs. From their perspective, they are the true leaders. Elijah, and the prophets, are radical, unreasonable, uncompromising troublers of Israel. They are not team players. No doubt Ahab and Jezebel could not understand why Elijah could not carry on a civil discussion about what they saw as tangential, civil issues. Likewise, recently our president was genuinely concerned that "conservatives cannot be civil and polite in their discussions about abortion." To many of us pro-lifers, and to Elijah, murder and apostasy do not engender etiquette.

This generation is the Elijah generation. To Elijah, the behavior of Ahab and Jezebel is absolutely appalling. While claiming to worship the Hebrew God, they also fill the land with syncretism, with apostate worship of the Baals. The crowning blow, to Elijah, is when these scoundrels placed the Asherah poles (places where believers could have sexual relations with temple prostitutes) on the hill next to the temple. Enough was enough and Elijah is ordered home to confront these evil powers on Mt. Carmel. And Elijah was not accommodating nor was he running away—don't you just wish, Ahab and Jezebel!—he is coming home to challenge the gods of this age.

Ahab and Jezebel are postmodernists. They celebrate the subjective. They are committed to compromise. Live and let live! What is the big deal? Well, you see, Elijah cannot compromise with the stuff they are doing. There is no wriggle room in Judah and there is getting to be precious little wriggle room in the U.S.A. too.

There is some good news here. The world of the Baals, folks, is falling apart. And quickly. As sociologist Peter Berger explains, "American mainline culture can no longer offer plausibility structures for the common man. It no longer sustains Americans." Or, as my old friend Professor Harvey Cox, at Harvard, coyly observed, "Once Americans had dreams and no technology to fulfill those dreams. Now Americans have tons of technology, but they have no dreams left."

In short order the Ahabs and Jezebels are going to find out that Elijah is not in a compromising mood either. Folks, there are some things one cannot compromise. Elijah and Jezebel are going to meet a man of God who speaks with concrete clarity, who carries the weight of truth. Elijah is coming, Christian brothers and sisters. The days of Obadiah are over. Elijah is coming to town.

Are you ready? Can you give up your anonymity? Will you risk everything this year to prepare this generation to be salt and light in a world that is losing its light and flavor? Will you go the extra mile in your home schooling to make sure that this generation will stand on Mt. Carmel and proclaim the sovereignty and goodness of our God? So they can bring the Kingdom on this earth as it is in heaven?

They cannot be simply good writers, they must be the best writers. They cannot merely pass through with an engineering degree. They have to be superb, gifted engineers. In the hallowed halls of Vanderbilt, Rutgers, and Harvard, it was my honor to learn with some of the greatest minds of my generation. I grew in Christ in the places. I prospered. I met my wife at Harvard. On Thursday night hundreds of strong believers gathered to lift up the name of God. But, slowly, year after year, enthusiasm waned. The exigencies of life took the fervor out of many of my friends' faith journey. It isn't that we all are not believers: we mostly are walking with the Lord. But what happened is that many of us were tamed, made impotent, by life itself. This must not happen with this generation!

The stakes are high; the potential rewards astounding. We have a chance, perhaps in our lifetime, to experience an unprecedented cultural revolution. In your homes are the new revolutionaries, who will go to the high places of this nation and proclaim the radical goodness of our God.

This is the generation of Elijah. The generation that will have to walk the long, arduous walk up Mt. Carmel and they will challenge the gods of this age. Bring it on! We are ready! Every knee shall bow, every tongue shall profess, that Jesus Christ is Lord. Bring on the fire of Elijah, again, on this nation! God is calling forth our children—Elijahs who will go to the high places of our nation to challenge the prophets of Baal— in the courts, in the university, in the shop, in the home, in churches.

Elijahs brought Good News but not welcome news. Good News that we gave them in our modest homes. Year after year, one music lesson after another, one coop meeting after another, one year after another, we raised this generation. And today, today they are on the threshold of changing their world. They are housewives, they have small businesses. They are writing scripts in Hollywood. Writing speeches for presidents. Lobbying for godly causes in Congress.

Do we have a vision of what lies ahead? Will we seek the Lord's face to cooperate in His equipping, enabling, and empowering process? Will we trust God? Elijahs are wild and crazy! They will move beyond our traditions and our comfort zones. Elijahs always do.

Challenge the gods of this age!

B. Augustine's *City of God* (AD 426), written at the very end of the Roman Empire, purported to prepare Christians to survive and even to prosper in the hostile environment that they would encounter with the collapse of the Roman Empire. If you accept that Christians are now a minority in America, explain how we can prepare to survive and thrive in this inhospitable, post-Christian era? **(25 points)**

Answer: Whatever a person or a nation sows, so shall he/it reap. Without a doubt, nations that ignore the precepts of the Lord shall ultimately fail. A cursory look at history confirms this: Babylon, Rome, and even Israel.

Chapter 12

ROMAN LIFE

First Thoughts . . .

The Roman Empire was more than ostentatious emperors and gladiator games. It was full of that people who had hopes and dreams similar to those which any people would have. The average Roman family consisted of father, mother, children, married sons and their families, and slaves. Women were married at about age 14 and died before they were 30. Men rarely lived to see their 40th birthday. There was no dating or courtship—the father of the family made all important decisions. In the midst of those trying times there were always the gods and the games. Romans loved their religion and their gladiator contests.

Chapter Learning Objectives . . .

As a result of this chapter you should be able to:

1. Compare and contrast Sumerian, Egyptian, Athenian, and Roman families.
   Answer Assignment 1

2. Pretend that you are an early Christian in Rome and speculate as to ways by which you might encourage these polytheists to become Christians.
   Answer Assignment 2

3. Analyze why Rome experienced comparatively few slave rebellions.
   Answer Assignment 3-A

4. Discuss why Roman Christians objected to slavery.
   Answer Assignment 3-B

5. Evaluate why the gladiator games were an accurate metaphor for Roman culture.
   Answer Assignment 4

6. Compare and contrast the Roman Empire with our "American Empire" of the 21st century.
   Answer Chapter Exam

ROMAN FAMILY LIFE

Assignment

Compare and contrast Sumerian, Egyptian, Athenian, and Roman families.

Answer:

	Sumerian Families	Egyptian Families	Athenian Families	Roman Families
Gender Roles	While women were honored, they did not have equal rights with males.	Until the time of Cleopatra, women were generally not allowed to be in places of influence.	While women were honored, they did not have equal rights with males.	While women were honored, they did not have equal rights with males.
Education	Upper-class males were educated. Women learned roles and skills at home.	Upper-class males were educated. Women learned roles and skills at home.	Upper-class males were educated. Women learned roles and skills at home.	Upper-class males were educated. Women learned roles and skills at home.
Religion	Sumerian society was polytheistic with Marduk as its primary god. It mostly practiced worship in homes, but priests at Ziggurats sacrificed to the gods. Sumerian religion did not promote any particular ethical code.	Egyptian society was mostly polytheistic— although for a while Amon-Ra alone was worshiped. It mostly practiced worship in homes but priests at temples sacrificed to the gods. Egyptian religion did not require any particular ethical behavior.	Athenian society was polytheistic. Religion was very much on the fringe of life. While Athenians were very superstitious, they did not espouse any creed or confession. Religion was very much a personal affair. Athenian religions were not in any sense ethical.	Roman society was polytheistic until the reign of Emperor Constantine. Religion was very much on the fringe of life. Religion was very much a personal affair, although most Romans during the Empire worshiped the Emperor. Roman religions were not in any sense ethical.
Occupation	All occupations were represented in Sumerian society.	All occupations were represented in Egyptian society.	All occupations were represented in Athenian society.	All occupations were represented in Roman society.

ROMAN RELIGION

Assignment

Pretend that you are an early Christian in Rome. You are preparing an evangelism campaign. What are some methods you might use to encourage these polytheists to become Christians?

Answer: The most compelling Christian witness would require no words or writings. One could show by actions and lifestyle the superiority of the Christian walk. This author would pray fervently for his Roman neighbors and look for opportunities to share Christ with them. Inevitably there would be opportunities. Health and financial crises occur in every person's life. This author will silently be prepared to share Christ with his neighbors during these times.

LESSON 3

ROMAN SLAVERY

Assignment

A. While slave rebellions occurred, there really were not very many of them. Why?

Answer: While slavery was brutal, slave rebellions were rare. Why? For one thing, the punishment for a slave rebellion was awful—crucifixion. This was a visible warning to recalcitrant slaves. Next, many slaves were from foreign nations. Even if a slave could escape, how could he return to his country? Finally, other than Spartacus there were very few slaves/leaders who would be willing to lead a rebellion.

B. Why did a number of Roman Christians object to slavery?

Answer: Some (not all) Roman Christians objected to slavery because it was inhumane, an impediment to evangelism, and a violation of the spirit (but not the literal) Word of God. While slavery was allowed in biblical times, it was not encouraged and it seemed to violate the free agricultural labor movement that characterized most of early Jewish and Christian farms. While there was no canonized Scripture as we know it, slavery, to many Christians, seemed to violate the spirit of the Pauline Epistles (the earliest available portions of Scripture).

LESSON 4

THE COLISEUM AND GLADIATORS

Assignment

Why were the gladiator games an accurate metaphor for Roman culture?

Answer: The Romans inherited the practice of gladiatorial games from the Etruscans, who used them as part of a funeral ritual (servants would duel to the death for the right to provide companionship to their owners in eternity). The first gladiatorial games were started in Rome in 264 BC by sons of Junius Brutus Pera in their father's honor after he had died. Gladiatorial combat became a very popular form of public spectacle very quickly in Rome. Julius Caesar promised 320 matches in funeral games for his daughter, Julia, but, to stop Pera, the Senate passed legislation limiting the amount of money that could be spent on gladiatorial games. Thus, during the Republic, gladiatorial combat was associated in Rome with death and elite competition. Such displays provided members of the elite with a vehicle with a means to influence the masses. It was, then, in a Roman way, like the present cash rebates that Congress gives to citizens to gain their support. In a way, then, the gladiator games were a metaphor for what was most "Roman" about the Roman Empire.

Essay Questions: 100-150 Words (100 points)

Some scholars compare the ancient Roman Empire to our "American Empire" in the 21st century. What similarities and differences can you identify? In your answer, include discussions about religion, the family, entertainment, and the military.

Answer: Rome was the most influential cultural influence for over 1,000 years. Likewise America is the most powerful and influential cultural influence in the world. Americans are enjoying an unprecedented time of peace. Pax Americana is used to describe a relative military peace in the Western world, resulting from the power enjoyed by the United States of America starting around the end of World War II. Certainly today America is indisputably the most powerful nation on earth. America's cultural impact is everywhere. American TV, American movies, and American fashion dominate world culture. Likewise Roman fashion and culture dominated the Western world. A play was first popular in Rome and then it was popular in Alexander. Romans wore a certain toga and it would inevitably reappear on people in Jerusalem. American pop icons such as Elvis Presley, Michael Jackson, Bona, and Madonna are global celebrities. Virgil was a "rock star" in his own right. America remains the most influential political, military, and social force in the world. Even when Roman political hegemony declined in the fourth century AD, its cultural influence remains even today. Finally, Rome and America were both very religious nations. During the Republic in particular, no Roman official could hold office if he did not uphold the highest moral standards. Likewise, America insisted upon high moral standards from its leadership. In both cases, in Rome and in America, the disappearance of high moral standards among public officials bodes poorly for the future.

Chapter 13

ROMAN THOUGHT AND DECLINE

First Thoughts...

The British historian Edwin Gibbon begins his epic *The Decline and Fall of the Roman Empire* this way: "In the second century of the Christian era, the Empire of Rome comprehended the fairest part of the earth, and the most civilized portion of mankind. The frontiers of that extensive monarchy were guarded by ancient renown and disciplined valor. The gentle but powerful influence of laws and manners had gradually cemented the union of the provinces. Their peaceful inhabitants enjoyed and abused the advantages of wealth and luxury. The image of a free constitution was preserved with decent reverence: the Roman senate appeared to possess the sovereign authority, and devolved on the emperors all the executive powers of government. During a happy period (AD 98–180) of more than fourscore years, the public administration was conducted by the virtue and abilities of Nerva, Trajan, Hadrian, and the two Antonines." Gibbons argues that the decline and fall of 1,000-year-old Rome occurred within the two generations—"a revolution which will ever be remembered, and is still felt by the nations of the earth." Why?

Chapter Learning Objectives...

As a result of this chapter you should be able to:

1. Identify an American author who has extolled America as Virgil in his writings extolled the Roman Empire.
   Answer Assignment 1

2. Discuss the ultimate outcome of a life focused on pleasure.
   Answer Assignment 2-A

3. Evaluate Stoicism.
   Answer Assignment 2-B

4. Explain why Neo-Platonism was such a threat to Christianity.
   Answer Assignment 3

5. Identify the factors that caused the fall of the Roman Empire.
   Answer Assignment 4

6. Reflect on the state of the "American Empire."
   Answer Chapter Exam

LESSON 1
VIRGIL

Assignment

Virgil's *Aeneid* follows the Trojan warrior Aeneas as he carries his family from his destroyed home, stops in Carthage for a doomed love affair, visits the underworld, and fights difficult battles in Italy. Finally, Aeneas founds Rome. Virgil was the national poet, the champion of Roman expansion. In the 21st century, does America have a "Virgil," an author who encourages patriotism? Who? Why do you choose this person?

Answer: Actually it is hard to find an author like Virgil in America today. While some artists/authors are outwardly supportive of some candidates, particularly liberal candidates, in fact, upon further examination, it appears that these same artists/authors are mostly self-centered and narcissistic. For example, the American president elected in 2008 appeared to have unanimous media and artistic support; however, as his administration unfolded, the fickle liberal artistic community, and to a lesser degree the media, more or less abandoned him. No, the author sees no Virgil in American society today. America needs a Robert Frost, Carl Sandburg, or Walt Whitman, all of whom extolled the American nation.

LESSON 2
EPICUREANISM AND STOICISM

Assignment

A. What is the ultimate outcome of a life that is focused on pleasure?

Answer: Ultimately the wages of sin is death. Period. A life focused on anything other than the person and works of our Lord, and His Word, will lead to destruction.

B. The Stoics had much truth: Life should be lived simply and completely. However, what is the thing that gives life ultimate and eternal meaning?

Answer: The thing that gives life ultimate and eternal meaning is a relationship with God. Other things, even good works, are superfluous.

LESSON 3
NEO-PLATONISM

Assignment

Neo-Platonism, with its emphasis on the supernatural, was a real threat to early Christianity. What contemporary religions and philosophies compete with Christianity?

Answer: Neo-Platonism, with its emphasis on the supernatural, was a great threat. It satisfied much of the spiritual needs of the waning years of the Roman Empire. At the same time, however, it offered no practical, human value to its followers. For example, Neo-Platonism had no ethical system to offer its followers. There was no example to follow as in our Lord Jesus Christ. Therefore, Neo-Platonic adherents found themselves feeling good, but not having any practical way to implement their religion into their lives. Today, Buddhism and Taoism make similar claims of Neo-Platonism and offer the same unsatisfactory ethical components.

LESSON 4

THE FALL OF ROME

Assignment

What caused the fall of the Roman Empire?

Answer: Historians argue that Christianity, moral decadence, and military problems caused the fall of Rome. Executive incompetence could be added to the list. Even the rise of Islam is proposed as the reason for Rome's fall, by some who think the Fall of Rome happened at Constantinople in AD 1453. To this author, the two that seemed to matter the most were moral decline and the weakening of the military.

EXAM KEY

Matching (50 points)

A. Romulus and Remus	E. Roman Monarchy	I. Augustus
B. Etruscans	F. Roman Republic	J. Constantine
C. Punic Wars	G. Spartacus	K. Goths
D. Hannibal	H. Julius Caesar	L. Roman Empire

E 1. The earliest period of Rome.

G 2. The leader of a great slave rebellion.

F 3. The time of democratic government in Roman history.

I 4. The emperor leading Rome during its golden age.

D 5. Carthaginian leader.

J 6. The emperor who made Christianity the most favored religion.

K 7. A barbarian people who twice attacked Rome and ultimately conquered it.

L 8. The last period of history in which dictators were the authorities in Rome.

H 9. The first Roman emperor.

B 10. The first civilization living in the Tiber area where Rome was founded.

A 11. Legendary founders of Rome.

C 12. Three Roman conflicts with Carthage.

Essay Questions: 80-100 Words (50 points)

With virtually no explanation, the author Edith Hamilton finished her book *The Roman Way* with this statement: "Material development outstripped human development." What do you suppose she meant?

Are we living during the end of the "American Empire"? Defend your answer.

Answer: Hamilton is right. The Roman Empire conquered the entire Western world, but its cultural strengths could not sustain this empire. While Roman hegemony brought order and stability everywhere, its moral, political, and religious dogma was bankrupt. This ultimately caused the collapse of the Roman Empire. Likewise, American society and culture is declining in influence. At the same time that American influence is at its apex, our Christian heritage is being diluted and compromised. This presages an ultimate collapse as surely as the moral and cultural degradation of Roman society presaged the collapse of the Roman Empire.

Chapter 14

EARLY CHURCH HISTORY

First Thoughts . . .

Christianity began as a small Jewish sect in the eastern Mediterranean region. It quickly grew in size and influence over a few decades, and by the fourth century AD had become the dominant religion within the Roman Empire. Today it is the most populous religion in the world. Why? How could a group of ordinary people such as fishermen and tax collectors, in one generation, turn the world upside down?

Chapter Learning Objectives . . .

As a result of this chapter you should be able to:

1. Discuss God's judgment.
   Answer Assignment 1-A, 1-B

2. Explore the difference between the public and the private lives of Christians.
   Answer Assignment 2-A, 2-B

3. Evaluate the impact of church buildings on Christianity.
   Answer Assignment 3-A

4. Gauge the impact of Constantine on church history.
   Answer Assignment 3-B

5. Discuss why Christians are such available targets for political leadership of a hosting country.
   Answer Assignment 4-A, 4-B

6. Evaluate the importance of Christians making decisions that may lead to persecution.
   Answer Chapter Exam

LESSON 1

THE BIRTH OF THE CHURCH
Assignment

A. Gnosticism, a particularly dangerous and effective first-century heresy, argued for a fundamental dualism between good and evil and salvation through "gnosis" or knowledge. What are contemporary manifestations of that heresy?

Answer: Many worship on the altar at the university. At the University of Pittsburgh, for example, the most important building on campus is the Cathedral of Learning. Interesting. Any culture that worships at the altar of knowledge is in big trouble.

B. One early Christian Gnostic, Marcion (AD 165), argued that Jesus was not really a man, but was instead a god in human "garb." What is the danger of advancing such a view?

Answer: If Jesus was not a man, and only a God, then He did not really suffer and die for human sins. Therefore, there is no expiation of sins, and no redemption. The incarnation is central to the redemption of mankind.

LESSON 2

THE NEXT CENTURY
Assignment

A. The early church welcomed everyone, male and female, Gentile and Jew. As a result, it was perceived as a radical body. How has the church today lost some of its radicalness?

Answer: In first-century society, it was expected that husbands would have one wife but many mistresses. Women expected this. Husbands could legally abuse their wives. Women expected this to occur too. Even though these problems destroyed families, infidelity and abuse were tolerated. Suddenly, a new group, a new religion preached monogamy and fidelity. To many women it was too good to be true! Nonetheless, it was true and women flocked to this new faith. The first-century Christian Church was not afraid to implement radical and controversial policies. Today, unfortunately, the Church follows societal trends, instead of implementing new, radical ones. This has been the case in the American Church for at least 50 years. Martin Luther King, Jr., in his Letters from a Birmingham Jail, warned the American Church that it had to embrace biblical truth, however radical and controversial it might be, or it would lose its relevancy and allure in modern society.

B. In AD 39–40, Philo of Alexandria (15 BC–AD 50) led a Jewish contingent to ask Emperor Caligula (AD 37–41) to end the persecution of Jews in Egypt. Caligula refused to listen to Philo, who later told his fellow ambassadors that God would punish Caligula. Not long after that, Caligula was assassinated. Does God punish people in this way?

Answer: Answers will vary. This author believes that He does but not because Philo says He does. His Word teaches us that the wages of sin is death. God is omnipotent and His Word is immutable. People do not break God's laws; they break people. Thus rulers who disobey God will ultimately be punished and even destroyed (e.g., Ahab and Jezebel, Herod, et al.).

CHRISTIANITY AND ROME

Assignment

A. In AD 231, in defiance of Roman law, a private house in the city of Dura-Europas on the Euphrates River was opened for Christian worship. No legal Christian church building was built and occupied for another 100 years. What effect did the inability to build/own church buildings have on the early Church?

Answer: Answers will vary. This historical truth forced the Early Church to be a small, dynamic, and neighborhood family unit. Churches were not encumbered with building maintenance and supervision. At the same time, churches remained small and personal. As a result, they were, in short, effective discipleship agents.

B. Constantine required everyone—Christian and pagan alike—to cease all work on Sunday in order to honor the Lord. Was Constantine correct in doing this?

Answer: Probably not, but it was a good idea. It certainly encouraged the serious pursuit of biblical truth! However, legislating morality is a very tenuous affair at best.

LESSON 4

MARTYRS

Assignment

A. Emperor Decius (249–251) required that everyone possess a certificate proving he had sacrificed to the gods. Some Christians either made sacrifices or purchased certificates of sacrifice from commissioners, which caused many believers to criticize them for "selling out" to the Romans. Some other believers argued that it was no big deal; that sacrificing to gods or buying a certificate under false pretenses really didn't matter. Still other believers argued that it was no one else's business what they did. What do you think?

Answer: Answers will vary. This is a tough one! While I agree that one should not sign the certificate— surely it is a big deal—and while I hope that I would be counted among those who refused to sign, I am unwilling to say that repentant brothers should be driven from the church. On the contrary, it seems to me that they have to be forgiven.

B. In February, AD 303, when augurs could no longer find the usual signs on the livers of sacrificed animals, Emperor Diocletian consulted the oracle of Apollo at Miletus, who said that the gods blamed the Christians.

At this provocation, Emperor Diocletian started a genocide campaign that nearly wiped out Christians. Why are Christians such available targets for political leadership of a host country?

Answer: Historically Christians have been an available, visible, pacifist minority who were easily identified and martyred. Therefore, hostile governments are quick to isolate and to persecute this group.

C. During the Diocletian persecution, a young Christian woman—Pelagia of Tarsus—refused to marry an unbeliever—one of Emperor Diocletian's sons—even though she was fond of him and he was in love with her. Despondent because he couldn't marry Pelagia, Diocletian's son committed suicide. Diocletian then had Pelagia burned at the stake. Was Pelagia right in making her decision? Would marrying Diocletian's son really have been such a big deal? What would you have done?

Answer: Answers will vary. As tragic as this story is, Pelagia obeyed Scripture, which commands that Christian believers should not be married to unbelievers.

EXAM KEY

Questions: 60-100 Words

A. Mani (216–274) was the founder of Manichaeanism, a religion that argued that matter is intrinsically evil, the prison of the soul. Salvation was through gnosis, an inner illumination in which the soul gained knowledge of God. The righteous went to paradise at death, but the wicked were reborn to live another life. This religion was very popular among intellectuals (e.g., Augustine followed Manichaeanism before his conversion). Why? **(34 points)**

Answer: It had a very high view of people. It also made salvation open to anyone who could "know" something rather than know someone. Thus, "salvation" required no behavior change or extraordinary commitment.

B. Pope Leo I (440–461) exhorted the Church to desist from mixing Christianity with sun worship. For instance, he rebuked his flock for paying reverence to the Sun god on the steps of St. Peter's before entering the basilica. How do contemporary Christians mix their faith with other religions? **(33 points)**

Answer: When Christian believers exhibit fear they succumb to the spirit of this age. Likewise, when they pursue money and power over the Kingdom of God they are paying reverence to the sun gods. Believers must be in the world, but not of it. Those who do not know the Word of God often mix other religious ideas into their Christianity, ideas picked up from media, friends, books, etc.

C. Heresy is more an excess of good theology than an aberration of bad theology. Explain what this statement means and agree or disagree with it **(33 points)**.

Answer: Inevitably some Christians take "good" theology too far. For instance, God is the provider of all good things. Likewise, it is important for Christians to have faith. However, to suggest that "faith" generates a blessing from God is a stretch. The "claim it and possess it" movement makes such a claim.

Chapter 15

CHRISTIANITY SPREADS

First Thoughts . . .

Old Testament Levitical priests had a duty to tend the fire in the tent of meeting, to keep it roaring and bright. The sacred fire was to be safe but huge. The fire on the altar, the eternal flame on which sacrifices were offered to God, was not to go out. Other duties could slide; other tasks could be deferred; but the fire on the altar was never to go out. At all costs and inconvenience, they were to preserve this sacred fire where God's people came to offer their gifts and rededicate themselves to Him.

Throughout the centuries, believers have served well as fire tenders. Brother Lawrence, Martin Luther, and others fanned the flames and kept the fire burning. "The secret things belong to the LORD our God, but the things revealed belong to us and to our children forever, that we may follow all the words of this law" (Deut. 29:29). This is a gathered inheritance kept alive by men and women of faith. We will look at that gathered inheritance together and thank God for the generations of faithful Christians who came before us.

Chapter Learning Objectives . . .

As a result of this chapter you should be able to:

1. Analyze Celsus' criticism of Christianity and Origen's refutation.
   Answer Assignment 1-A, 1-B

2. Analyze how Christians can remain relevant in the contemporary world without compromising the integrity of their faith.
   Answer Assignment 1-C

3. Appraise the importance of Benedict to church history.
   Answer Assignment 2

4. Evaluate the importance of Josephus' writings.
   Answer Assignment 3

5. Observe the impact of unforgiveness on world history.
   Answer Assignment 4

6. Delineate how Christianity emerged from Judaism and maintained its integrity as a movement.
   Answer Chapter Exam

LESSON 1

A GATHERED INHERITANCE

Assignment

A. What was Celsus' criticism of Christianity and what was Origen's refutation?

Answer: Celsus claimed that signs and wonders occurring in Christian churches were demonic. Origen reminded his opponent that these miracles were the result of providential activity—not demonic activity. For one thing, these miracles bring good things into the human community. Satan would never do that.

B. Origen was a man fervently committed to the cause of Christ. Yet, as often happens, many of his followers misunderstood Origen and corrupted his message. How can we be faithful to the gospel, yet try to ensure that our followers will not corrupt what we say?

Answer: This is a difficult thing. One can hope that humility and prayer will ensure the longevity and integrity of the Christian movement.

C. What does Benedict mean when he says "the heart becomes broadened"?

Answer: By practicing spiritual disciplines, believers enjoy an enlarged and more effective Christian walk. All of this largesse is connected to a committed life of connecting their lives more fully to the person of Christ.

LESSON 2

A BOOK REVIEW

Assignment

In these early years of the 21st century, the emerging post-Christian world is challenging Christians in unprecedented ways. Yet, there is value in looking again at the Early Church. What can contemporary Christians learn from the Early Church that can help us survive and thrive in our unbelieving, often hostile world?

Answer: The Early Church was able to effectively survive, to prosper, in a hostile culture by the Word of God, by the Blood of the Lamb, and being willing to give their lives for the Truth (Revelation 12).

Assignment

Josephus wrote, "Now there was about this time Jesus, a wise man, if it be lawful to call him a man; for he was a doer of wonderful works, a teacher of such men as receive the truth with pleasure. He drew over to him both many of the Jews and many of the Gentiles. He was [the] Christ. And when Pilate, at the suggestion of the principal men amongst us, had condemned him to the cross, those that loved him at the first did not forsake him; for he appeared to them alive again the third day; as the divine prophets had foretold these and ten thousand other wonderful things concerning him. And the tribe of Christians, so named from him, are not extinct at this day." Why is Josephus' extra-biblical description so important to the authentication of the origins of Christianity?

Answer: The unsaved, objective historian Josephus confirms several claims of the gospel. Jesus Christ existed. He was a Jew and lived among the Jews. He died on a cross and His followers thrived.

Assignment

When Augustine was a bishop in the Roman Catholic Church, Christians were facing terrible persecution by the Romans. Many—actually most—of the priests and other leaders of whom Augustine had charge denounced their faith. When the persecution ended, many former leaders repented and were reinstated in the Church. However, the Donatists rejected this decision and founded their own church. Donatists were North African believers who, despite losing loved ones to torture and death, had not given in to persecution and no longer wanted to be associated with a church whose leaders had caved in when faced with persecution. Were the Donatists right or wrong in their decision? Why?

Answer: While readers can sympathize with the Donatists, unforgiveness is a very dangerous thing. The Bible teaches that if believers wish to be forgiven, they must first forgive. The Donatists, in effect, formed a "root of bitterness" and the Church, once powerful and numerous in North Africa, basically disappeared.

EXAM KEY

Questions: 60-100 Words

A. Philo was also a theologian who sought to harmonize Jewish theology with Greek (largely Platonic) philosophy. In today's vernacular, Philo tried to make Judaism "modern" by harmonizing it with secularism. Later Christian theologians (e.g., Origen) tried to do the same thing. Is it possible to make the Christian message more "modern" without compromising its integrity? If not, why? If so, how? **(34 points)**

Answer: Answers will vary. The Christian faith presumably needs to be reinterpreted in every generation to its world. However, the Word never changes.

B. The theologian/church father Ignatius claimed that the bishop was God's representative on earth. In a letter to the Ephesians, Ignatius wrote, "Be ye subject to the Bishop and Presbytery. . . . For even Jesus Christ, our inseparable Life, is the manifest Will of the Father; as also Bishops, to the uttermost bounds of the earth, are so by the will of Jesus Christ." In light of the view of the doctrine of the priesthood of all believers (see Rev. 1:4–6), do you agree or disagree with Ignatius? Explain your reasoning **(33 points)**.

Answer: This reader is not prepared to take issue with Ignatius, but certainly spiritual leaders should be God's representatives. This author would not go so far as to suggest that they speak for God in all things at all times.

C. In AD 127–142, Ptolemy, a committed Christian and astronomer, postulated that the earth was the center of the universe. This view held until 1542, when Copernicus supplied a solar-centered model. While Ptolemy's view seemed to concur with Orthodox Christianity, from the beginning there has been a tension between faith and science. What is this tension and how can it be resolved? **(33 points)**

Answer: The notion of the "sphere of influence" does not work. This position argues that science and faith should be separate. Such views are preposterous—since so much science is another form of faith. For instance, evolution requires more "faith" than creationism. So, the fact is, since the Word of God is infallible and inerrant, if the Bible says that the sun stopped when Joshua fought a battle, then most assuredly it happened the way the Bible said it did, regardless of scientific theory or plausibility issues.

Chapter 16

JAPANESE HISTORY

First Thoughts . . .

The word "Japan" does not appear in history until AD 57 when it is first mentioned in Chinese histories. The Chinese historians tell us of a land divided into 100 or so separate tribal communities without writing or political cohesion. The Japanese are latecomers in Asian history. These warrior people ultimately dominated all of Asia. Where did the Japanese come from? Why did they settle on the islands? What was life like for them?

Chapter Learning Objectives . . .

As a result of this chapter you should be able to:

1. Identify historical trends that emerged from the beginning of Japanese history.
   Answer Assignment 1

2. Understand the role that the Samurai assumed in Japanese society.
   Answer Assignment 2

3. Discuss several Christian objections to Buddhism.
   Answer Assignment 3-A

4. Define Shintoism and discuss why it thrived in Japan.
   Answer Assignment 3-B

5. Analyze why Japanese women produced more art than their Western counterparts.
   Answer Assignment 4

6. Explain why Japanese ballads celebrated only regal subjects.
   Answer Chapter Exam

LESSON 1

EARLY JAPANESE HISTORY
Assignment

What historical trends emerge from the beginning of Japanese history?

Answer: Japan is an anachronism. On one hand Japan is steeped in tradition; on the other hand it is a very progressive country. The existence of a samurai leadership cadre and a culture that encourages hard work assured Japanese industrial hegemony.

LESSON 2

THE EMPEROR
Assignment

Who were the samurai and what role did they assume in Japanese society?

Answer: A warrior class that evolved into the elite of Japanese culture. The warriors were typically landholders—many, minor landholders, yeoman farmers, really. They were not necessarily rich noblemen. They lived in small, fortified compounds, and they offered the surrounding peasant communities succor and protection. Often warriors served as local district officials, judges, even priests, but they remained quintessential warriors. Much of their time was devoted to the cultivation of warfare. As a result, they were extremely effective administrators and warriors. With their land holdings, military skills, and administrative skills, the warriors were a powerful presence in Japanese society.

LESSON 3

JAPANESE RELIGIONS
Assignment

A. What are several Christian objections to Buddhism?

Answer: Buddhists do not believe in heaven or in an eternity anywhere for that matter. They believe that by following the teaching of Buddhism strictly and leading a perfect life they will escape a cycle of rebirths and cease to exist. This end to the soul is called Nirvana. It might seem hard to believe that anyone would look forward to a gift of nothing, but it's important to understand that family traditions, an attachment to earthly pursuits and worldly pleasures, and a strong disbelief in God can blind them to how much better the hope Christ gives us is. Use your personal experiences and your own life as an example of the hope they can have. But, also keep in mind many Buddhists will look at Christians who are wrapped up in worldly things as an example of Christianity and they may not understand how people so focused on their earthly lives could really believe in a better place.

B. What is Shintoism and why did it thrive in Japan?

Answer: Shintoism was a religion that encouraged worship of ancestors. By the 16th century a religious movement called Shintoism dominated Japanese culture. The Tokugawa "Enlightenment" inspired a group of thinkers who tried to define the essential Japanese character as it existed before it was tainted by foreign influence. It was a concerted philosophical effort to reclaim what was distinctively "Japanese." Shintoism sought to purge Japanese thought of Confucianism (Chinese), Taoism (Chinese), Buddhism (Indian and Chinese), and Christianity (Western European). Shintoism fit very well into the Samurai system. For one thing, Shinto followers worshiped clan ancestors. Ancestors were revered and emulated. Shinto followers worshiped at a shrine—one of the first Asian religions that promoted a significant cultic location to revere the gods. Shintoism, in summary, was a philosophy/religion whose gods were male family ancestors. The local family/clan was the most important building block in Japanese culture. The reputation of the family was the avowed responsibility of every clan member. Death was preferred to bringing dishonor to the family name.

LESSON 4
JAPANESE LITERATURE

Assignment

Japanese women produced more art than their Western counterparts. Why?

Answer: Most of the women who produced this art were mistresses and concubines of wealthy Japanese nobility. European monogamous Christian nobility did not participate in such a lifestyle. At the same time, Japanese culture encouraged the production of poetry both as a hobby and as a religious discipline.

EXAM KEY

Questions 60-100 Words (50 points each)

A. In ancient Europe there were several tales such as *Beowulf* and *The Song of Roland* whose heroes were courageous and bold. At the same time, ballads emerged that described the lives of common people (e.g., "The Ballad of Robin Hood"). In contrast, Japanese ballads rarely extolled the lives of common people. Rather, they celebrated the exploits of the kings and the deeds of heroes. Why?

Answer: Japanese culture extolled the extraordinary and empathic. Earthy, entertaining ballads would be beneath the dignity of Japanese patrons.

B. Roman Catholicism had a great impact on European ancient life. Likewise, Shintoism and Buddhism impacted Japanese life in a different way. How?

Answer: Roman Catholicism was highly institutional and impacted secular government in an indelible way. It had a strict liturgy and demanded that everyone participate in weekly services. Finally, Roman Catholicism advanced a Judeo-Christian morality that impacted all of European society. Shintoism and Buddhism had no such effects on Japanese society. Shintoism and Buddhism, which some detractors call a form of "atheism," merely encourages a higher consciousness with very few moral/ethical demands on their followers.

Chapter 17

INDIAN (SOUTH ASIAN) HISTORY

First Thoughts . . .

Mark Twain quipped, "India is the cradle of human race, the birthplace of human speech, the mother of history, the grandmother of legend, and the great-grandmother of tradition. Our most valuable and most astrictive materials in the history of man are treasured up in India only!" The Indus River Valley civilization began in India around 2500 BC. From this auspicious beginning, Indian people groups spread over, and conquered, the South Asian subcontinent.

Chapter Learning Objectives . . .

As a result of this chapter you should be able to:

1. Discuss historical trends that emerged in Indian history.
   Answer Assignment 1

2. Identify at what point India gained a national identity.
   Answer Assignment 2-A

3. Contrast the British invasion of India with other invasions.
   Answer Assignment 2-B

4. Describe the challenges Thomas encountered in taking the gospel to India.
   Answer Assignment 3

5. Discuss why a Christian would want to study Hinduism.
   Answer Assignment 4

6. Analyze how Indian culture was connected to Hinduism.
   Answer Chapter Exam

Assignment

What historical trends emerged in Indian history?

Answer: Very early religion (i.e., Hinduism) was tied to India's national identity. It defined its national identity. Thus, Christianity and Islam were more than a threat to its religious underpinnings; it was a threat to its national identity. This did not change until the emergence of the secular Indian state after World War II. This does, however, partly explain the conflict that exists between Islamic Pakistan and Hindu India. Another historical trend: India is at the crossroads between the East and the West. It was always embraced for its military value, although it was also quite difficult to conquer (with its natural boundaries, e.g., the Himalayan Mountains).

Assignment

A. At what point did India have a national identity?

Answer: The Aryans helped this occur, but the emergence of Hinduism was a defining moment. Religion ultimately formed the nation that emerged. Religion defined and encouraged the caste system. With society being divided on the basis of castes, conflicts and disorders were bound to arise. A need arose, therefore, for a strong external force to enforce these divisions and to arbitrate these conflicts. This gradually led to full-fledged state systems, including vast empires.

B. In what ways was the British invasion of India different from other invasions?

Answer: The British did not wish to assimilate with the Indians; they merely wished to control its resources and they wished to bring them home. The British did not want to create colonies as they had done in America and Australia. They merely wanted to trade. In order to do so, the British saw that they had to conquer the country.

Assignment

What challenges did Thomas encounter when he brought the gospel to India?

Answer: Hinduism, the primary religion in India, and the greatest competitor to Christianity, was indelibly tied to Indian culture. To attack Hinduism was to attack what was most "Indian" about Indian culture.

LESSON 4
INDIAN RELIGIONS
Assignment

Why would a Christian want to study Hinduism?

Answer: Hindus generally do not refer to their goal as "salvation." The hope is to escape the reincarnation cycle and material existence. Other terms are used for it. Anything that pertains to leaving this material life or moving beyond it is commonly said to be "transcendental." (This term is used repeatedly in the introduction to the Bhagavadgita.) There are several ways taught by which this can be done. One way is good deeds. If Hindus do enough good works, especially works that are unselfish and de-emphasize material interests, they will achieve a better reincarnation. This process continues till finally one escapes reincarnation and material existence completely. There are several other ways that Hindus can be saved. One can withdraw from the pleasures and personal interests of life. By studying the Vedas, a Hindu comes to understand that his true nature is part of the Diving Being. As he fills his mind with such ideas, his thoughts and deeds are less concerned with material interests. When he dies, physical life has no power over him, so he is released. In all these avenues, repeated reincarnations may be required as a person gradually moves to higher and higher levels till he leaves the cycle. He must bring this about by his own effort. The gods may help, but there is no concept of a Supreme Being who pays the penalty of sin on behalf of the sinner. By understanding what is lacking in Hinduism, Christians can share the Good News of God, who not only made a way for eternal salvation but who also invites present relationship in the midst of daily life. Hindus do not enjoy personal relationships with any of their myriad of gods and goddesses.

EXAM KEY

Questions: 80-100 Words (100 points)

One historian claims that it is impossible to understand Indian history unless one understands Hinduism. Even Christians, they argue, are affected by "Hindi culture." Agree or disagree and give reasons for your opinion.

Answer: At the heart of Indian culture is Hinduism. Its caste system, its pursuit of pleasure and restraint (both at the same time) create the heart and soul of India.

Chapter 18

PERSIAN HISTORY

First Thoughts . . .

The Persian Empire was the largest known empire. It gave southwestern Asia and adjoining regions an unprecedented degree of organization. The Persians built roads and established the first important postal system in history to maintain communication between the emperor and his commonwealth. Known for their religious tolerance, the Persians respected the traditions of the people they conquered, as in allowing the Israelites to rebuild their holy city of Jerusalem. Through Judaism and, later, Christianity, Persia's Zoroastrian faith would have a powerful if indirect effect on the spiritual life of the West. All of this was to change with the advent of Islam, which was neither tolerant nor enlightened. The Persians, now called the Iranians, entered a sort of Dark Age.

Chapter Learning Objectives . . .

As a result of this chapter you should be able to:

1. Explain what historical trends emerge in Persian history.
   Answer Assignment 1

2. Discuss why the Islamic invasion threatened Persian society and culture.
   Answer Assignment 2-A

3. Tell what two European powers had designs on Iran/Persia and why.
   Answer Assignment 2-B

4. Speculate upon why Manichaean religion is so popular today.
   Answer Assignment 3

5. Explore legends about the wise men from the East.
   Answer Assignment 4

6. Describe what historical trends emerge in Persian history.
   Answer Chapter Exam

LESSON 1

ANCIENT PERSIA

Assignment

For more than 3,000 years Persia was a melting pot of civilizations and demographic movements between Asia and Europe. Under Cyrus the Great, it became the center of the world's first empire. Successive invasions by the Greeks, Arabs, Mongols, and Turks developed the nation's culture through rich and diverse philosophical, artistic, scientific, and religious influences, but Persia was still able to maintain its national identity. What historical trends emerge in Persian history?

Answer: Persia was between the East and the West—it was juxtaposed between two super-powers (Rome-China, Russia-England). Therefore, its future, to a large degree, was determined by outside influences. Resentment grew and ultimately married itself to nationalism that emerged in the 20th century. Iran, for instance, became an increasingly isolationist and anti-foreign influence. Persia was able to maintain its identity through religion.

LESSON 2

ISLAMIC KINGDOMS

Assignment

A. Why did the Islamic invasion threaten Persian society and culture?

Answer: Islamic faith is an exclusive, intolerant religion. It rejected everything Persian, in other words, and it was a difficult job for a Persian to maintain his identity. Nonetheless, Persian culture filtered into the modern Iranian state.

B. What two European powers had particular interest in Iran? Why?

Answer: Britain wished to increase trade opportunities, particularly for opium. Russia wished to have a warm water port.

LESSON 3

MANICHAEAN RELIGION

Assignment

The Manichean cult has experienced a comeback in the last few years. Why do you think Manichaeism would be so popular among contemporary people?

Answer: The notion that "knowledge" or "gnosis" brings salvation is naturally popular in a culture that worships human progress and knowledge. At the heart of this view is the Platonic notion that somehow knowledge and ethics are connected.

Assignment

Why is the biblical account of the wise men an important part of the Christmas story?

Answer: Traditionally the account of the wise men is an indicator of Christ's influence on non-Jews or Gentiles. Jesus was to be the Savior of all people, Jews and Gentiles.

EXAM KEY

Question: 80-100 Words (100 points)

There is a Persian Proverb that says, "History is a mirror of the past and a lesson for the present." How does Persian history mirror those words?

Answer: Persia, at the crossroads of Europe and Asia, was a critical player in the development of Indo-European civilizations. For 3,000 years the Persian court held cultural and political hegemony over half a continent. Ironically, it was a religious power (Islam) rather than a political power that conquered Persia, and the country that emerged—modern Iran—now perceives its Persian heritage as "pagan." This is a mirror of the past. This in no way mitigates the impact that the Persians had, and still have, on Indo-European culture as it emerges in the 21st century. This is the lesson for the present and future.

Chapter 19

CHINESE HISTORY

First Thoughts . . .

Chinese civilization began around 2500–2000 BC, about 1,000 years earlier than Western European civilization (1000 BC) and more than 3,000 years before European-American civilization (AD 1600). A rich culture thrived in the lower Huang He (Yellow River) Valley of northern China. What makes the civilization unique in world history is its continuity through more than 4,000 years. No other civilization can make that claim! The Chinese kept voluminous records from the beginning. The strange thing is that throughout China's history, its scholars alluded to its cultural separateness from its contiguous neighbors. Thus, Chinese people, it seems, have always had a sense of their unique cultural identity.

Chapter Learning Objectives . . .

As a result of this chapter you should be able to:

1. Compare Chinese civilization with European civilization, c. AD 500–1000.
   Answer Assignment 1

2. Delineate historical trends that emerge in Chinese history.
   Answer Assignment 2

3. Evaluate Communism's appeal to the Chinese people.
   Answer Assignment 3-A, 3-B

4. Predict the future of the People's Republic of China.
   Answer Assignment 3-C

5. Explain why Daoism would work better in a totalitarian regime than in a democracy.
   Answer Assignment 4-A

6. Explore why Confucius, who never claimed to be a deity and never set out to found a religion, became, after his death, both a deity and the focus of a religion.
   Answer Assignment 4-B

7. Discuss why European technology quickly surpassed Chinese technology.
   Answer chapter Exam A, B

Assignment

The Shang king's rule was based equally on religious and political power. He played a priestly role in the worship of his ancestors and he was the political leader of China too. Compare this leadership paradigm with what emerged in Europe, c. AD 500–1000.

Answer: Early European leaders were respectful, even fearful, of the Church, i.e., the Roman Catholic Church. But the priest was always separate from the civil leadership. There was no serious notion of a "divine ruler" in early Europe (although this concept existed in Roman history and some European monarchs made this claim). Cultic leadership and political leadership were separated in European politics; it was not the case in China.

Assignment

What historical trends emerge in Chinese history?

Answer: Early 21st-century Chinese society has developed out of some 3,300 years of history. For these 3,000 years China progressed form dynasty to dynasty until it reached the present Communist Republic. The following factors more or less determined Chinese history:

1. The vastness of the land. China is a huge geographical area.

2. Aggressive neighbors. China has few natural, physical barriers to its neighbors. Thus, it had to build things like the Great Wall.

3. Large population. China's ready labor supply delayed the industrial revolution until the 20th century.

Assignment

A. Why did Communism appeal so strongly to the Chinese people?

Answer: It is a religion that fared well in the peasantry. It purported to "empower" the disenfranchised masses of which China had a surplus.

B. Based on the past, what do you think the future holds for the People's Republic of China?

Answer: Answers will vary. China, though, is clearly becoming increasingly "Westernized." In order to enter and to complete in the international community, China has had to mitigate some of its Communist excesses.

C. Technology played a key role in military and political victories that emerged in early Chinese history. Compare that to the geopolitical situation that exists today.

Answer: Today the United States has military supremacy partly as a result of our technological superiority. This technology may or may not be connected to an altruistic political system. For instance, Nazi Germany was technologically the most advanced nation in the world at the beginning of the World War II, but it certainly did not represent a high moral position.

LESSON 4

CHINESE RELIGIONS

Assignment

A. Why would Daoism work better in a totalitarianism regime than in a democracy?

Answer: Daoism is a form of stoicism that invites its followers to discipline, hard work, and contentment in whatever situation a follower finds himself. It also celebrates tradition and ancestry.

B. Why would a person like Confucius, who never claimed to be a deity and never wanted to found a religion, become, after his death, both a deity and the focus of a religion?

Answer: Great leaders, especially great religious leaders, become larger than life after their death. Confucius, like Socrates and Jesus, wrote nothing. But his followers extolled his virtues and his wisdom and, in effect, deified him. Confucius never sought, and in fact would have been appalled, at this unsolicited approbation.

EXAM KEY

Questions: 60-100 Words (50 points each)

A. In spite of China's strong beginning, why did European technology quickly surpass Chinese technology?

Answer: One impetus for European industrial expansion was a shortage of labor. China never experienced this shortage and had no reason to encourage industry. Also, Daoism encouraged an agrarian lifestyle and discouraged an urban, industrial lifestyle. Thus it amazed early Europeans that the Chinese had very little interest in European goods. Why, then, would they need industries?

B. To many ancient Chinese authorities, the arrival of Buddhism from India was perceived as a religious and political threat. Indeed, many Daoist and Legalist Chinese officials saw it as a threat to everything dear in their culture. Today, some Americans are similarly concerned about the growth in America of such religions as Islam, Hinduism, and Buddhism. They are afraid that these religions are a threat to America's unique culture. Explain why you agree or disagree with their assessment.

Answer: Answers will vary, but in a nation that was founded on religious freedom we are on shaky ground if we define any one religion as an "American" religion. That does not, however, change the fact that America was founded by Judeo-Christian colonists.

Chapter 20

THE MIDDLE AGES

First Thoughts . . .

While the Sui Dynasty ruled in China, in Europe, in AD 410, Alaric, king of the German Visigoths, led his army into northern Italy. The Visigoths had come to ask the Roman authorities to grant their people land. The Romans ignored Alaric's request and he destroyed Rome. As the Roman Empire collapsed, Europe entered a vast and varied period of history commonly referred to as the Dark Ages. The Early Middle Ages saw the continuation of trends set in Late Antiquity—depopulation, a slowing of urbanization, and increased barbarian invasion. North Africa and the Middle East, once part of the Eastern Roman Empire, were conquered by Islam. Later in the period, the establishment of the feudal system allowed a return to systemic agriculture. There was sustained urbanization in Northern and Western Europe. During the High Middle Ages (c. 1000–1300), Christian-oriented art and architecture flourished and Crusades were mounted to recapture the Holy Land. The influence of the emerging nation-state was tempered by the ideal of an international Christendom. The codes of chivalry and courtly love set rules for proper behavior, while the Scholastic philosophers attempted to reconcile faith and reason.

Chapter Learning Objectives . . .

As a result of this chapter you should be able to:

1. Evaluate Marco Polo's impact on medieval history.
   Answer Assignment 1-A

2. Contrast the life of a typical noblewoman with that of an average peasant woman.
   Answer Assignment 1-B

3. Discuss the Saracens and their threat to Europe.
   Answer Assignment 1-C

4. Explain how religion and superstitions mixed during the Middle Ages.
   Answer Assignment 2-A, 2-B

5. Reflect upon the impact of St. Francis on world history.
   Answer Assignment 3

6. Evaluate the pros and cons of Scholasticism.
   Answer Assignment 4

7. Understand the impact of the Middle Ages on world history.
   Answer Chapter Exam A, B

END OF AN EMPIRE TO THE REFORMATION

Assignment

A. Marco Polo described the attempt to invade Japan by Kublai Kahn, whose efforts were thwarted when his ships were destroyed by a typhoon. This "Divine Wind" or "Kamikaze" was a term resurrected by the Japanese during World War II to describe their pilots who flew suicide missions against American naval ships. Does God intervene, as Marco Polo supposed, on the side of one army or another in a conflict? Give reasons for your opinion.

Answer: In most cases, there are Christian believers living in adversarial nations. Therefore, it is quite problematic to claim that God supports one group of Christians against another. Look at the last portion of Joshua chapter 5. A similar question is asked. So perhaps the question is not concerning God taking sides, but "Who is on the Lord's side?"

B. Contrast the lives of a noblewoman and a peasant woman in the Middle Ages.

Answer: Medieval society would have been very traditional. The primary role of noblewomen and peasant women were to support their husbands, to maintain the household, and to raise the children. But their work did not end there. Within a village, women would have done many of the tasks men did on the land. However, they were paid less for doing the same job. About 90 percent of all women lived in rural areas and were therefore involved in some form of farm work. Laws greatly limited the freedom of all women. Women were

- not allowed to marry without their parents' consent;

- not allowed to divorce their husbands;

- could not own property of any kind unless they were widows.

Many women from rich backgrounds would have married when they were teenagers. Children from poor families would have worked from the earliest age possible, and they were treated as adults from the age of ten or eleven. Many girls from poor families did not get married until they were in their twenties. They were needed in their father's home. Women had no choice over who they married, and many girls from rich families were usually married to someone as a political gesture. Producing a male heir within a rich family was considered vital. So many women spent a great deal of their married life pregnant. However, childbirth was dangerous as medical care was so poor. It is thought that as many as 20 percent of all women died in childbirth, and it was the most common cause of death among young women. Wives from a rich family usually did not look after their children. This was done by a helper. Women from a poor family not only had to look after the children but had to continue doing her day-to-day work both in the home and on the land. Many women from poor families did not live past the age of 40.

C. Why were the Saracens such a great threat to Medieval Europe? What do you think would have happened if they had succeeded in conquering all of Europe?

Answer: The Saracens were followers of Mohammed and Islamic people groups were intolerant of Christians. Europe might well have been a predominantly Islamic region if the Saracens had succeeded in spreading across Europe.

THE ROMAN CATHOLIC CHURCH

Assignment

A. Civilizations as early as the Chaldeans in southwestern Asia were among the first to claim spiritual belief in plants that never existed—a practice that continued during the Middle Ages. One of the most amazing beliefs was that a tree existed that had barnacles that opened to reveal geese. Why were such explanations presented and why did people believe them?

Answer: In a pre-scientific world these folk tales were plausible explanations to describe natural phenomena.

B. Important in the celebration of Christmas was the banquet, which varied in generosity according to the resources of the celebrants. Churches and houses were decorated with ivy, mistletoe, holly, or, for the first time, with a Christmas tree. The gift-giving of the season was represented by the New Year Gift, which continued a tradition of Roman origin. The later Christmas present was not part of a Medieval Christmas. In fact, the Medieval Christmas was an eclectic event. What part of Christmas was Christian and what part was pagan?

Answer: The celebration of the birth of Christ was of course "Christian." But that was about it. The Christmas tree, holly, mistletoe, etc., all had pagan roots.

FRANCIS OF ASSISI

Assignment

Describe a humble Christian who, perhaps unknown to other people, has had a positive impact on the world.

Answer: Answers will vary.

SCHOLASTICISM AND ERASMUS

Assignment

A. The Scholastics tried to argue from rationalism that God exists and that He is omnipotent. Why is this so difficult?

Answer: Scholasticism emphasized dialectical (rational argumentation) reasoning; they gave a new direction to Christian tradition in philosophy. However, the key components of Christianity cannot be understood rationally: things like love, faith, and hope.

B. Erasmus suggested something that was innocuous enough: that people should primarily be concerned with their happiness. Why is this a dangerous notion?

Answer: Erasmus was a certifiable genius. He translated the New Testament and wrote other important works. Erasmus, as opposed to Aquinas and the Scholastics, emphasized the empathic to the exclusion of the rational. In fact, the chief end of man is to love God and to enjoy Him forever. The rational will not take one to God.

EXAM KEY

Questions: 60-100 Words (50 points each)

A. Why is it incorrect to call the Middle Ages the "Dark Ages"?

Answer: As one historian explains, "The Dark Ages were a tumultuous time. Roving horse-bound invaders charged the countrysides. Religious conflicts arose; Muslims conquered lands. Scarcity of sound literature and cultural achievements marked these years; barbarous practices prevailed." In reality, though, the Middle Ages were anything but dark. Some Protestants called this time "dark" because of the corruption of the Roman Catholic Church. But that was shortsighted. While there was corruption, this was the time that many magnificent cathedrals were built. The irony of this is that our 21st-century world is no less dark. It feels a lot like we are living in a post-Christian, dark age!

B. Bubonic Plague started in China and made its way west across Asia to the Black Sea by 1347. One theory is that a group of infected Tartars besieged a Genoese outpost on the coast. To harass the trapped townspeople, the Tartars used their catapults to hurl the dead bodies of their comrades over the town walls, spreading the epidemic among the Genoese. The panicked inhabitants fled the scene by ship, showing up in the ports of northern Italy and bringing the Black Death to Europe. Why was the Bubonic Plague so difficult to contain?

Answer: No one knew what caused it. As a result no one could offer interventions. Often poor choices were made. For example, the Plague was carried by mice and rats. In some cities, superstitious churchmen, blaming feline morphed witches, killed all the cats in the city! This of course caused the Plague to spread even more.

Chapter 21

THE CRUSADES

First Thoughts . . .

Regarding the Crusades of the 11th through the 13th centuries, G. K. Chesterton wrote, "High ideas were besmirched by cruelty and greed, enterprise and endurance by a blind and narrow self-righteousness, and the Holy War itself was nothing more than a long act of intolerance in the name of God, which is a sin against the Holy Ghost." Some people, however, do not share his negativity. The late Dr. Bruce Shelley, a staff member of *Christianity Today* magazine, wrote, "Many Muslims, for instance, still reckon that the crusades initiated centuries of European aggression and exploitation. Some Catholics want the Pope to apologize to the world for them. Liberals of all stripes see the crusades as examples of bigotry and fanaticism. Almost all these opinions are, however, based on fallacies. The denigrators of the crusades stress their brutality and savagery, which cannot be denied; but they offer no explanation other than the stupidity, barbarism, and intolerance of the crusaders, on whom it has become conventional to lay most blame. Yet the original justification for crusading was Muslim aggression; and in terms of atrocities, the two sides' scores were about even." What really happened in the Crusades? Why did they occur?

Chapter Learning Objectives . . .

As a result of this chapter you should be able to:

1. Understand the causes and results of the Crusades.
   Answer Assignment 1-A, 1-B, 1-C

2. Discuss the views of Christians and Islamic people concerning the Crusades.
   Answer Assignment 2-A, 2-B, 2-C, 2-D

3. Discuss the lives of Christian European women in the Crusades.
   Answer Assignment 3

4. Evaluate the views of the philosopher Francis Bacon.
   Answer Assignment 4

5. Examine when or if ever the Christian should force his faith on others.
   Answer Chapter Exam A, B, C

CAUSES AND RESULTS

Assignment

In AD 637 Islamic general Caliph Omar conquered the city of Jerusalem, the center of the Christian world and a magnet for Christian pilgrims. The city's Muslim masters exhibited religious tolerance. No new churches were to be built, and crosses could not be publicly displayed outside church buildings, but the pilgrims were allowed to continue their treks to the holiest shrines of Christendom (although they were charged a toll). Things stayed the same for more than 400 years. Then, in the latter part of the 11th century (1076), Turkish Muslims conquered Jerusalem. Now, vicious attacks were waged on the Christian pilgrims and their sacred shrines in the Holy City. The Holy Land was now in the smothering grip of infidels, and the Europeans determined that something had to be done. In response, Pope Urban II called a conference at the city of Clermont, France, in 1095, and exhorted the assembled multitude to wrest the Holy Land from the hands of the Muslims, assuring them that God would absolve them from any sin associated with the venture. The First Crusade was the most successful in that it actually accomplished what it set out to do—conquer Jerusalem. But it had its problems. Led by Peter the Hermit and Walter the Penniless, one poor group marched across Europe to Constantinople, only to be slaughtered by the Turks soon after crossing into Asia Minor. What was the allure of a "Crusade" to otherwise poor pilgrims?

Answer: Pious motivations plus the allure of international travel. Remember, too, the papacy announced that sinners could be assured of eternal salvation if they participated in a Crusade. To a population who considered age 40 to be an old age, a sure ticket to eternal bliss was a pretty appealing option.

OPPOSING VIEWS OF THE CRUSADES

Assignment

A. Would Pope Urban's arguments persuade you to join the Crusade? Why? Why not?

Answer: Answers will vary. This reader might be persuaded. Since I would live only until I was 35 or 40, and who knows where I would spend eternity (Roman Catholic theology was not as full of assurance on the topic as later Protestant theology), I might very well take up Pope Urban's offer that any crusader was guaranteed a ticket to heaven! Besides, it might gaul me that the sacred Christian sites were being abused by Islamic infidels!

B. Why was Mullah Mohammed Ben Zeky so pleased that the Christian "infidels" had been defeated?

Answer: How cruel and unforgiving some of the Christian Crusaders were! Zeky met some of these. Some Crusaders mercilessly murdered vanquished foes, women and children included. That is not to say that excesses did not occur on both sides. In this case, though, Mullah Mohammed Ben Zeky saw the Christians as barbarians and, in truth, there was some justification for his judgment.

C. In the spring of 1097, a host of more than 100,000 crusaders joined forces on the eastern side of the Bosporus. The combined army then fought its way along the coast of the Mediterranean, reaching the gates of Jerusalem in June of 1099. The following is a contemporary account of the capture of Jerusalem:

Exulting with joy we reached the city of Jerusalem on Tuesday, June 6, and we besieged it in a wonderful manner. . . . During the siege we were unable to find any bread to buy for about the space of ten days, until a messenger came from our ships; also we were afflicted by great thirst, so much so that in fear and terror we had to water our horses and other animals six miles away. The fountain of Siloam, at the foot of Mount Zion, sustained us, but the water was sold among us at a high price. . . . We sewed up skins of oxen and buffaloes in which we brought the water six miles. The water we drank from such receptacles was fetid, and what with foul water and barley bread we daily suffered great affliction and distress. Moreover the Saracens hid near all the springs and wells and ambushed our men, killing and mutilating them and driving off the animals into their dens and caverns. Then our leaders planned to attack the city with machines, in order to enter it and adore the sepulcher of our Savior. They made two wooden towers and many other machines. . . . Day and night on the fourth and fifth days of the week we vigorously attacked the city on all sides; but before we made our assault the bishops and priests persuaded all by their preaching and exhortation that a procession should be made round Jerusalem to God's honor, faithfully accompanied by prayers, alms, and fasting. Early on the sixth day we attacked the city on all sides and could do nothing against it. We were all surprised and alarmed. Then, at the approach of the hour at which our Lord Jesus Christ deigned to undergo the passion of the cross for us, our knights in one of the towers fought bravely, amongst them Duke Godfrey and his brother, Count Eustace. One of our knights climbed on to the wall of the city. When he reached the top, all the defenders of the city quickly fled along the walls and through the city. Our men followed and pursued them, killing and hacking, as far as the temple of Solomon, and there was such a slaughter that our men were up to their ankles in the enemy's blood. . . . The emir who commanded the tower of David surrendered to the Count [of St. Giles] and opened the gate where pilgrims used to pay tribute. Entering the city, our pilgrims pursued and killed the Saracens up to the temple of Solomon. There the Saracens assembled and resisted fiercely all day, so that the whole temple flowed with their blood.

In what ways is this account encouraging and, at the same time, shocking?

Answer: This reader does not find this account encouraging at all. It was so violent and senseless. And a terrible witness to the God this reader serves!

D. In the year 1187, the Muslim leader Saladin conquered the city of Jerusalem as well as most of the Crusader strongholds throughout the Holy Land. In response, the kings of Europe, including Frederick Barbarossa of Germany (who died en route), Philip II of France, and Richard I (the Lion-Hearted) of England mounted a campaign to rescue the city. The Third Crusade was underway. The key to the campaign's success was the capture of the port city of Acre. King Richard arrived on the scene in June 1191 to find the city under siege by a Christian army. Intensifying the bombardment of the city, Richard and the French king, Philip, slowly broke the city's walls, weakening its defenses while simultaneously starving the occupiers into submission. Finally, on July 12, the Muslim defenders and Crusaders agreed to surrender terms. In exchange for sparing the lives of the defenders, Saladin would pay a ransom of 200,000 gold pieces, release some 1,500 Christian prisoners, and return the Holy Cross. These actions were to be accomplished within one month after the fall of the city. Richard would hold 2,700 Muslim prisoners hostage until the terms were met. Saladin immediately ran into problems completing his part of the bargain. The deadline came without payment of the terms. Saladin offered a compromise. Richard refused to compromise and declared the lives of the Muslim defenders of Acre forfeit.

The following is an eyewitness account of the slaughter of 2,500 captives:

"Then the King of England, seeing all the delays interposed by the Sultan to the execution of the treaty, acted perfidiously as regards his Islamic prisoners. On their yielding the town he had engaged to grant their life, adding that if the Sultan carried out the bargain he would give them freedom and suffer them to carry off their children and wives; if the Sultan did not fulfill his engagements they were to be made slaves. Now the king broke his promises to them and made open display of what he had till now kept hidden in his heart, by carrying out what he had intended to do after he had received the money and the Frank prisoners. It is thus that people of his nation ultimately admitted. The King ordered all the Islamic prisoners, whose martyrdom God had decreed for this day, to be brought before him. They numbered more than three thousand and were all bound with ropes. The Franks then flung themselves upon them all at once and massacred them with sword and lance in cold blood."

Was this slaughter justified? What damage resulted from this decision at that time and in later years?

Answer: Certainly the slaughter was not justified. Such behavior gave Christianity a very bad reputation in the Middle East.

LESSON 3

QUEEN ELEANOR OF AQUITAINE

Assignment

If you were a mother or a wife of a Crusader, why would you want to accompany your son or husband?

Answer: We have virtually no record of the effect of the Crusades on families, but it certainly would have been difficult to see one's spouse disappear for three to five years, the average duration of a Crusade.

Assignment

What does Bacon mean when he implies that scientific knowledge may lead to salvation, but the prerequisite for this revealed wisdom of science is Christian morality? Why is that a dangerous thought?

Answer: This is a precursor to thought advanced by David Hume and is dangerous because salvation is a free gift of God given as we confess Jesus Christ as Lord. It actually is a very unmeasurable, abstract concept—not a "natural law" or a scientific concept.

EXAM KEY

Questions: 60–100 Words

A. In a broad sense, the Crusades were an expression of militant Christianity and European expansion. While the original purpose of the Crusades was religious, it quickly became secular. The Crusades combined religious interests with secular and military enterprises. In many ways this was a disconcerting beginning. Why? **(33 points)**

Answer: Pope Urban II's original intent was to reclaim the Holy Land for pilgrims. Only later were colonization and other agendas added to the equation—and these were added by secular interests.

B. Under what, if any, circumstances should Christians pressure others to embrace the Christian faith? **(33 points)**

Answer: This reader cannot imagine that that would ever be a viable, moral, ethical option! We must be careful to allow the Holy Spirit to be the one to convict and convert. Jesus invited sinners to "see" the Father when He perfectly represented the One who sent Him.

C. What impact did the Crusades have on Western Europe? **(34 points)**

Answer: The Crusades were of course military failures. On the other hand, the Crusades made Western Europe more cosmopolitan. Perhaps the Crusades also brought Europe out of the end of the Dark Ages. The most important effect of the Crusades was economic. The Italian cities prospered from the transport of Crusaders and replaced Byzantines and Muslims as merchant-traders in the Mediterranean. It also provoked such Atlantic powers as Spain and Portugal to seek trade routes to India and China. Their efforts, through such explorers as Christopher Columbus, opened most of the world to European trade dominance and colonization and shifted the center of commercial activity from the Mediterranean to Central Europe.

Chapter 22

AGE OF DISCOVERY

First Thoughts . . .

The mid-to-late 15th century has quite rightly been called the Age of Discovery. It was an age in which European ships left the safe coastal waters of the Old World and embarked on their adventures to the New World. First, Portuguese ships, then Spanish, and, in the late 15th and early 16th centuries, British, French, and Dutch ships set out to discover a world that they originally called the Other World—the Indies—but eventually called the New World. The truth is, the costs were minimal but the risks were high. Whole continents were discovered and explored. Why did Europeans take to the oceans beyond their nearby seas? What made the civilizations of the Renaissance turn to discovery? The main motive was economic. Europeans recognized that the Far East was rich in luxuries. One shipload of trade goods from the "Indies" (which we call China) could make a man wealthy for the rest of his life.

Chapter Learning Objectives . . .

As a result of this chapter you should be able to:

1. Discuss the factors that prompted two centuries of exploration.
   Answer Assignment 1, Chapter Exam A, B

2. Explore the Huguenot persecution.
   Answer Question 2-A, 2-C, 2-D

3. Analyze the cause of religious persecution.
   Answer Question 2-B

4. Evaluate what makes a primary source reliable.
   Answer Question 2-E

5. Understand why Portugal led Europe in the initial stages of exploration.
   Answer Assignment 3

6. Compare different world views that emerged in the 16th century.
   Answer Assignment 4-A, 4-B

7. Explain how the Crusades were connected to the Age of Discovery.
   Answer Chapter Exam C

DISCOVERY AND EXPLORATION

Assignment

What prompted two centuries of European exploration?

Answer: In the second half of the 15th century, European sailors began to plan voyages that would take them beyond the limits of the world they knew. The new interest in the world came in part from the Renaissance, but the main reason was to set up new trading links with spice-producing lands in Asia. Profit was the main impetus. One overland caravan or shipload of East Indian spices would make an investor fabulously wealthy.

RELIGIOUS PERSECUTION

Assignment

A. In the Huguenot passage, who is the speaker? Why would he refer only to Roman Catholics as Christians?

Answer: He is a Spanish Roman Catholic but even he was horrified by the slaughter of Huguenots that occurred in Florida. To this pious Roman Catholic, Protestants were not Christians.

B. How do you react to the speaker's statement that the Holy Spirit led his group to trick and then massacre the Protestants?

Answer: While the author does not doubt the speaker's sincerity, he cannot believe that the Holy Spirit would do any such thing.

C. If you had been a Huguenot in the situation described, would you have quickly converted to save your life?

Answer: Answers will vary.

D. Why do some Christians kill one another "in the name of Christ"?

Answer: No doubt the Roman Catholic perpetrators did not see the Huguenots as "Christians" or they would not have killed them. Nonetheless, it is interesting that Spanish Roman Catholics were killing English Roman Catholics, and vice versa. Apparently the allure of a nation state was greater than the allure of the Kingdom of God.

E. Is the Magellan passage a dependable account of this event? Why or why not?

Answer: Yes. The speaker is a Venetian (Italian) who has no ulterior motive to present any particular viewpoint.

PRINCE HENRY THE NAVIGATOR

Assignment

In what way was Prince Henry the Navigator a history maker?

Answer: Despite the creation of the caravel and other technological advances and the knowledge shared at his school for sailors, Prince Henry had a great deal of difficulty persuading his captains to sail beyond Cape Bojodor off the west coast of Africa. According to legend, beyond this point in an area known as the "Green Sea of Darkness," the sun was so close to the earth that a person's skin would burn black, the sea boiled, ships caught on fire, and monsters hid waiting to smash the ships and eat the sailors. It took 14 voyages over a period of 12 years until a ship finally reached the equator. During the two-year period from 1444 to 1446, Prince Henry intensified the exploration of Africa, sending between 30 and 40 of his ships on missions. The last voyage sponsored by Prince Henry sailed over 1,500 miles down the African coast. Although he never sailed on the expeditions, the voyages that he paid for in the mid-1400s helped launch Portugal into the front of the race to find a sea route to the Indies. Later, sailors like Christopher Columbus were encouraged to travel even farther from European shores.

LESSON 4

MONTAIGNE AND HOBBES

Assignment

A. Is it possible to "suspend judgment"?

Answer: Michel de Montaigne made himself the great object of study in his essays. In studying himself, Montaigne is studying mankind. He attempted to weigh or "assay" his nature, habits, his own opinions and those of others. He was also a striking representative of Renaissance skepticism. Skepticism was the doctrine that knowledge about some particular topic was not possible, e.g., religion. Science was developing. New horizons made previous truths seem wrong or parochial. These discoveries provided Montaigne with new facts that made relative all beliefs. One had to "suspend judgment" to assume one's humble place in the universe. Can one suspend judgment? Montaigne would have us think that faith is an abstract notion that requires "suspension of judgment." No. That is not true. Like Plato, and his perception of the "form," the Christian understands that faith and love and hope and other godly principles are more real than anything else in the universe. One does not need, therefore, to suspend judgment to believe and practice them.

B. Why is Hobbes so popular among Marxist historians?

Answer: At the center of Marxism is the notion of the "struggle" between classes from which emerges a better world.

EXAM KEY

Assignment

A. Why did Portugal lead Europe in the initial stages of exploration? **(25 points)**

Answer: Thanks to Prince Henry the Navigator, Portugal was the leader in technology, mapmaking, and other necessary advances in exploration. Portugal also had the necessary capital to support exploration attempts. Prince Henry was the ramrod that make all this possible.

B. Discuss how the Crusades stimulated the Age of Discovery. **(25 points)**

Answer: After traveling to the Middle East, as the Crusaders came home, they yearned to explore and to own land that was far from European civilization.

C. Why did Europe send explorers east and west to find China, while China conducted no similar explorations? **(50 points)**

Answer: After the great Chinese Emperor Kublai Kahn, Chinese emperors looked inward, not outward, to further exploration. There were exceptions. From 1405 to 1433, a large fleet of Admiral Zheng traveled to the Western Ocean (the Chinese name for the Indian Ocean) seven times. This attempt did not lead China to global expansion, as the Chinese were content trading with already existing tributary states nearby and abroad. To them, traveling far east into the Pacific Ocean represented entering a broad wasteland of water with uncertain benefits of trade. Why travel to Europe when Europe was content to travel to China?

Chapter 23

THE RENAISSANCE

First Thoughts . . .

The mention of the Renaissance evokes images of nude human sculptures and realistic, brightly colored paintings. The modest, godly, unpretentious, halo graced paintings of the Middle Ages were in the past. "Renaissance" is the French term for "rebirth." Historians first used it in about 1840 to describe the period from the 14th to the 16th centuries, implying a rediscovery of rational civilization (exemplified by Greece and Rome) after the medieval centuries. The term "Middle Ages," also coined by historians, had a much more negative meaning. The truth is, it is impossible to establish clear dividing lines between medieval and Renaissance periods. In art (particularly sculpture), stylistic hints of the coming Renaissance appeared well before 1300, and the study of classical literature was well underway before the Renaissance began. Nonetheless, for our purposes, the Renaissance is the first modern era to dawn in the European pantheon.

Chapter Learning Objectives . . .

As a result of this chapter you should be able to:

1. Discuss the origin of the Renaissance and its implications for future generations.
   Answer Assignment 1-A, Chapter Exam Questions

2. Explore the link between the Renaissance and nationalism.
   Answer Assignment 1-B

3. Analyze Renaissance art.
   Answer Assignment 2

4. Explore the emergence of modern science during the Renaissance.
   Answer Assignment 3

5. Evaluate the works of Petrarch and Machiavelli.
   Answer Assignment 4

THE RENAISSANCE: PART ONE
Assignment

A. Scholar Jacob Burckhardt writes, "In the Middle Ages both sides of human consciousness—that which was turned within as that which was turned without—lay dreaming or half awake beneath a common veil. The veil was woven of faith, illusion, and childish prepossession, through which the world and history were seen clad in strange hues. Man was conscious of himself only as a member of a race, people, party, family, or corporation—only through some general category. In Italy this veil first melted into air; an objective treatment and consideration of the state and of all the things of this world became possible. The subjective side at the same time asserted itself with corresponding emphasis; man became a spiritual individual and recognized himself as such. In the same way the Greek had once distinguished himself from the barbarian, and the Arab had felt himself an individual at a time when other Asiatics knew themselves only as members of a race."

Paraphrase what Professor Burckhardt is saying.

Answer: Burckhardt suggests that in the Middle Ages humankind saw himself as a religious being, in that way was "dreaming or half awake beneath a common veil." Burckhardt is critical of this personae, which to him was "woven of faith, illusion, and childish prepossession." Suddenly, in Italy, during the Renaissance, humankind woke up and "man became a spiritual individual and recognized himself as such." Burckhardt, then, is very negative about the theistic vision of the Middle Ages and celebrates the humanism inherent in the Renaissance. This author disagrees with this view. The Renaissance vision, which, by the way, was not entirely "subjective" did not ameliorate the human condition. A walk with God, based on the Word of God, is the only real way to be truly happy and productive.

B. In the 14th and 15th centuries many Italian scholars became aware of history. One group of Italian writers in the 14th century emphasized that their age resembled the great Roman civilization of the past. They tried to incorporate these perceived similarities into their civilization. What are the dangers of doing this?

Answer: While it is quite harmless to replicate certain aspects of an earlier civilization, it can be dangerous to replicate all. There were great Roman civilizations in the past (e.g., Augustus) but there were also some very bad ones (e.g., Nero). One must be careful to replicate positive things from one without wandering into the latter. Also, living in the past ignores the real time challenges and opportunities of the present.

THE RENAISSANCE: PART TWO
Assignment

What ominous development occurred in Renaissance art?

Answer: For the first time the individual was studied and admired separate from his or her environment. Human relationships became paramount—the test tube environment in which one learned truth. Art, once reserved for the depiction of religious subjects, expanded to include ordinary people and objects. Thus, in the Renaissance painting *The Lovers*, a man and a woman, for one of the first time, are pictured in a romantic human relationship. Quite tame by today's standards, this piece was extremely controversial in 16th-century Europe.

HISTORICAL DEBATE

Assignment

Some Renaissance scholars thought that the emergence of modern science lay in a view of nature that was based on the ideas of Christian biblical witness. Such a view of the universe was essentially supernatural and could not be studied objectively or by experimentation. They introduced the concept of the universe as an entity that could be approached objectively. What is wrong with this view?

Answer: There is nothing objective about the universe—with love and purpose God Himself created the heavens and the earth. He is personally involved with His creation. He loved the world so much that He sent His only begotten Son to die for the sins of humankind. The Renaissance scholars, like the Greek empiricist Aristotle, tried to have their cake and eat it too. One cannot "suspend belief" so to speak and study science and then return hat in hand to God. For instance, either the creation narrative is historically accurate or it is not. It is a tenuous balance to be sure. "Such a view of the universe was essentially supernatural and could not be studied objectively or by experimentation." Yes, it can, later scientists discovered.

PETRARCH AND MACHIAVELLI

Assignment

A. What is Petrarch's point in writing to the dead Roman poet Cicero?

Answer: Because Petrarch's peers neither read or appreciated great orators like Cicero, "it is a great grief to me, a great disgrace to this generation, a great wrong done to posterity. The shame of failing to cultivate our own talents, thereby depriving the future of the fruits that they might have yielded, is not enough for us; we must waste and spoil, through our cruel and insufferable neglect, the fruits of your labors too, and of those of your fellows as well, for the fate that I lament in the case of your own books has befallen the works of many another illustrious man."

B. What advice does Machiavelli give potential rulers?

Answer: Machiavelli admits that cunning can accomplish more than sincerity. "Everyone understands how praiseworthy it is in a Prince to keep faith, and to live uprightly and not craftily. Nevertheless, we see from what has taken place in our own days that Princes who have set little store by their word, but have known how to overreach men by their cunning, have accomplished great things, and in the end got the better of those who trusted to honest dealing. Be it known, then, that there are two ways of contending, one in accordance with the laws, the other by force; the first of which is proper to men, the second to beasts. . . . But since a Prince should know how to use the beast's nature wisely, he ought of beasts to choose both the lion and the fox; for the lion cannot guard himself from the toils, nor the fox from wolves. He must therefore be a fox to discern toils, and a lion to drive off wolves."

EXAM KEY

Assignment (50 points each)

A. To our present-day hopeless, secular world, history is mundane; it is merely utilitarian. To Christians, history is sacred, fraught with opportunity. To secular people, history is not didactic; it helps people feel better. To Christians, history is full of important lessons, and it challenges people to be all they can be in Christ. To secular people, time and space are finite entities full of fearful pitfalls. To Christians, no matter how bad things are, because God is alive and well, time is holy and the land is holy. Secular people act out of no purpose or design. In contrast, Christians know that God is in absolute control of history. In a way that is not mawkish or condescending, Christians must be tirelessly hopeful. We can do that by speaking the truth of God's Word in places where truth is not recognized. Cite examples of how modern scholars, politicians, and philosophers are not fully appreciating history.

Answer: In the beginning of the 21st century President Obama instituted Depression economic principles that did not work in the 1930s and would not work in the 21st century. Likewise, the United States in its haphazard but inexorable rush away from its Judeo-Christian moorings could very well be doomed to decline as surely as other civilizations and empires have declined. Gibbons in his seminal study of the decline of the Roman Empire observed how great nations ignore the lessons of history at their own peril. The United States is in danger of creating the same mistake.

B. Every generation thinks that it does everything new—that it reinvents the wheel, so to speak. Certainly this was the case with my generation growing up in the 1960s. Compare and contrast your generation with the Renaissance generation.

Answer: In the beginning of the 21st century when postmodernism is very popular, there is a growing distrust of science. Postmodernism is as radical a shift in thought as the Renaissance. Postmodernism rejects objective truth and emphasizes the role of language, subjectivity, and motivations. Post-Modernist thought is an intentional departure from scientific approaches that had previously been dominant. The term "postmodernism" comes from its critique of the "modernist" scientific mentality of objectivity and progress associated with the Enlightenment and science.

Chapter 24

THE REFORMATION

First Thoughts . . .

In the middle of the 16th century, a Roman Catholic priest named Martin Luther became greatly distressed as he read in Paul's letter to the Roman Christians: "For in the [gospel], the righteousness of God is revealed from faith for faith, as it is written, 'The righteous shall live by faith'" (Rom. 1:17). Luther wrote, "I greatly longed to understand Paul's Epistle to the Romans and nothing stood in the way but that one expression, 'the righteousness of God,' because I took it to mean that righteousness whereby God is just and deals justly in punishing the unjust. My situation was that, although an impeccable monk, I stood before God as a sinner troubled in conscience, and I had no confidence that my merit would assuage Him. Therefore I did not love a just angry God, but rather hated and murmured against Him. Yet I clung to the dear Paul and had a great yearning to know what he meant." It was from this prayerful beginning that a movement aimed at reforming the Roman Catholic Church began. It eventually culminated in the establishment of Protestantism, which spread all over the world and changed history forever.

Chapter Learning Objectives . . .

As a result of this chapter you should be able to:

1. Analyze Martin Luther's influence on the Reformation.
   Answer Assignment 1-A

2. Consider the importance of the printing press on the Reformation.
   Answer Assignment 1-B

3. Discuss the power of prayer and its impact on history.
   Answer Assignment 2

4. Evaluate whether the Protestant Reformation was necessary.
   Answer Assignment 3

5. Test and weigh the veracity of the theories of Max Weber.
   Answer Assignment 4

6. Synthesize the causes of the Reformation into a succinct theory.
   Answer Chapter Exam Questions

LESSON 1

THE PROTESTANT REFORMATION
Assignment

A. Without a doubt Martin Luther was a mighty, anointed man of God. We Christians all owe him a debt of gratitude. However, Luther had a weak spot: he was avowedly anti-Semitic. Luther writes, "Therefore be on your guard against the Jews, knowing that wherever they have their synagogues, nothing is found but a den of devils in which sheer self-glory, conceit, lies, blasphemy, and defaming of God and men are practiced most maliciously and veheming his eyes on them." While many pious Christians shared Luther's views, it surely is grievous that this great man wrote such things. Why? How should Christians react to statements like this?

Answer: Luther was not perfect. Far from it. Unfortunately, like most of his Roman Catholic and Protestant peers, Luther was anti-Semitic. Christians should confront other believers when they exhibit this prejudice.

B. Without the printing press, John Dillinger argues, Luther would have been just another little-known Christian martyr. Why do you agree or disagree?

Answer: The printing press was an important ally to Luther. He could preach an important sermon one Sunday and by the next Thursday every European city could have a copy. The first printing press was invented by the German Johannes Gutenberg around 1440. His newly devised hand mold made possible for the first time the precise and rapid creation of metal movable type in large quantities, a key element in the profitability of the whole printing enterprise.

LESSON 2

NIKOLAUS VON ZINZENDORF
Assignment

Discuss an incident in your own life where your own prayers, or the prayers of others, changed your life.

Answer: Answers will vary. I have many examples of how prayer changed my life. Here is one. Once, for three years, I walked the halls of the place I worked (public school) and prayed that God would bring revival in this school. I told no one I was praying.

The first year violent attacks on teachers dropped 1000%. The next year the dropout rate went from 46% to 3%. The final year a Wednesday Bible study began. And no one ever knew that from 5:30 to 7:00 a.m. every morning I was walking the halls of this school and praying! To God alone belongs the glory.

LESSON 3

THE CATHOLIC COUNTER-REFORMATION
Assignment

Was the Protestant Reformation necessary? Why or why not?

Answer: The Protestant Reformation was a major 16th-century European reformation of the beliefs and practices of the Roman Catholic Church. It is the opinion of the author that this corrective was necessary. It seems unlikely that the Roman Catholic hierarchy would change some of its practices voluntarily. Besides, by the time the Reformation was over, many theological practices of the Roman Catholic Church were more than "corrected"— they were discarded (e.g., Indulgences). At the same time, some theological points were emphasized (e.g., the Priesthood of all Believers).

HISTORICAL ESSAY: MAX WEBER

Assignment

Agree or disagree with Weber's statement and defend your argument.

Answer: The reader only has to compare Protestant England, Germany, and the United States to Roman Catholic Spain, Italy, and France to see that Protestantism encouraged industrialism.

EXAM KEY

Questions: 60-100 Words

A. As a reporter for a newspaper, write an article on the Protestant Reformation. You are required to include the following topics **(60 points)**:

1. Causes of the Reformation
2. Key Figures: Calvin, Wycliffe, Erasmus
3. Similarities and differences between the Roman Catholic Church and the early Protestant Church
4. Results of the Reformation

Answer: Many scholars would set the dawn of the historical landmark of the Reformation on the shoulders of Martin Luther. Their focus would fall upon the nailing of his 95 Theses to the door of a church in Wittenberg as the inauguration for the Protestant. The Reformation actually began over 100 years before Luther was born. The first reformer to be noticed is John Wycliffe. He did not believe in the clerical ownership of land and property, as well as papal jurisdiction in secular affairs. He also believed that those clergy who lived in open immorality, as many of the corrupt "popes, bishops, and priests of the time," should relinquish their positions the moment they came upon unrepentant open sin.

The next great figure of Reformation thought (which at this time was simply an adherence to the truths of the Bible) was a Bohemian monk named John Hus (Jan Hus). He lived from 1372–1415. Hus preached against clerical abuses of power, immorality among the Catholic clergy, and the worship of the pope. He wrote to promote piety and godliness, rather than riotous living and excess, which the Roman Catholic Church seemed to allow.

After John Hus, the next noteworthy reformer is William Tyndale. He was born in AD 1493, and died a martyr in 1536. Tyndale secretly finished the translation with the help of colleagues, and smuggled the new translation into English hands. All of the above mentioned reformers, though, remained Roman Catholic. Martin Luther was the first Protestant. Luther, after his conversion, posted his 95 Theses to the door of a chapel in Wittenberg on October 31, 1517. This instigated a great controversy since he attacked the indulgences of the Roman Catholic Church (Matthew McMahon).

B. Many Christian scholars, including this author, feel that some Protestant reformers went too far in their protests against the Roman Catholic Church. What happens when a legitimate reform movement tries to overcome poor choices with equally poor ones? **(40 points)**

Answer: This reader is sympathetic with the Protestant response to 16th-century Roman Catholicism; however, one must never overcome evil with evil. One overcomes evil with good. If one does employ evil as a response to evil the outcome can be disastrous. For example, in Joseph Conrad's *Heart of Darkness* the protagonist Kurtz goes to Africa to enlighten the savages, but he himself becomes a savage! Pious Christians who overcome evil with evil become evil themselves. In the 16th century, and today, the majority of Christians are Roman Catholic! One must not judge a whole church by its excesses.

Chapter 25

THE FRENCH REVOLUTION

First Thoughts . . .

Less than a decade after the American Revolution, the French Revolution began. The French Revolution of 1789 began the Modern Era. In a sequence of upheavals, it saw the downfall of King Louis XVI, the rise of Robespierre, and the Reign of Terror, during which thousands were guillotined for political differences. Revolutionaries saw the Catholic Church as the enemy and promoted in its place a Cult of Reason. The Revolution emerged in part from the rationalism of the Enlightenment, which distrusted all established institutions. It inspired fear in European monarchs and aristocrats, as well as conservative intellectuals like Edmund Burke in Britain, who mobilized his pen to fight the Revolution.

Chapter Learning Objectives . . .

As a result of this chapter you should be able to:

1. Analyze the causes and results of the French Revolution.
    Answer Assignment 1

2. Discuss why bloody excesses occurred in the French Revolution.
    Answer Assignment 2, Chapter Exam

3. Evaluate the impact of Immanuel Kant on world history.
    Answer Assignment 3-A, 3-B

4. Judge the world views of several 18th- and 19th-century philosophers.
    Answer Assignment 4-A, 4-B

Assignment

Louis XVI did not want to be king. He was not equipped to be a good king. He became king by default. He was a man of Christian morals, yet he was a poor ruler. How could Louis have been expected to live up to the reputation of his father and grandfather who had ruled France when it was prosperous and strong? Do you think Louis XVI was a victim of circumstances or a major cause of the French Revolution? Why?

Answer: Pompous, irascible, vain to a fault, Louis XVI was consistently a loser. There was no hypocrisy in him. Nor was there much passion. There was nothing subtle about him either. There are sympathetic voices, though. Historian John Harman argues that the reign of Louis XVI, which ended in 1793 with the guillotining of the king and his queen, Marie-Antoinette, was a great tragedy and egregious mistake. But he was a dramatic and crucial part of French history. His account of the first

12 years of Louis's reign, from 1774 to 1786, reveals a capable king, especially in the fields of foreign affairs and public finance, but a stubborn king too. In response to the troubles in 1787–89 Hardman believes that Louis XVI was sincere. Finally, according to Hardman, Louis XVI emerged as a ruler with clear ideas and a genuine concern for the French people, even as he died as a "martyr" for the people. Most historians, however, agree with this author. In fact, historian Michael Walzer defends the trial and execution of Louis XVI as necessary, since it not only tried to destroy the monarchy's mystique and divine right, but also required the deputies to fully explain their guiding philosophies and applied the rules of judicial process to establish equality before the law.

Assignment

The French Revolution introduced a new type of personality: the self-confident, idealistic revolutionary. Maximilien Robespierre symbolized its extremes: laudable humanist ideology and cold-blooded murder. He not only encouraged the Reign of Terror, he created an ideological basis for its existence. What is most disconcerting about this era, and this man, is that Robespierre was seen by contemporaries as virtuous—a righteous man, bringing the vengeance of the Lord on scoundrels and rascally enemies of the Revolution. What causes a Judeo-Christians society, whose church attendance is almost 100 percent, to execute thousands of people in the name of justice? How can this "Christian" country have leaders like Robespierre?

Answer: Answers will vary. This reader agrees with historian Ruth Scurr, who argues that Robespierre evolved from a shy, provincial lawyer to a ruthlessly efficient, revolutionary leader, righteous and paranoid in equal measure. She argues that he spread himself too thin and had visions of grandeur—he was sure that he could do it all: build a

Republic and even found a new religion. In this time of unrest and confusion, Robespierre was a clear voice who couched his policy in liberal, revolutionary language. Like Thomas Paine, his friend, he espoused the laudable goals of equality and justice for all, but inherent in their views was a covert intolerance of anyone who disagreed with them. France created a "Robespierre." It needed a leader whose voice exhibited revolutionary idealism and religious zeal. Christian nations in crisis, like France in 1789 and Germany in 1932, forget, overlook, or ignore biblical principles to embrace a sense of false security.

LESSON 3

IMMANUEL KANT
Assignment

A. Immanuel Kant was identified by some of his Christian contemporaries as being a serious threat to Christianity. Why?

Answer: Truth, to Kant, was limited to irreducible human-created structures. Morality and ethics would never be a priori truth. With only a priori knowledge, Kant argued, morality was based on man's ability to act rationally, not on any ipso facto phenomenon. The human mind actively shapes sensations into ideas by selecting and coordinating them according to certain ordering principles, e.g., space and time. Thus, space and time are random principles, because the mind cannot organize sensations without reference to these categories. Yet human reason gives us no access to the "thing-in-itself": We have access only to our experience of the thing. There is no objective reality, then, in Kantian philosophy. Therefore, the Bible—the penultimate objective source of Truth—has no authority in the philosophy of Immanuel Kant.

B. Why is Kant's philosophy so popular today?

Answer: The predominant philosophy in the first few decades of the 21st century is called postmodernism. Postmodernism rejects objective truth and celebrates subjectivity. It emphasizes the role of language and motivations; in particular it pronounces as irrelevant any dialectic categories such as male versus female, straight versus gay, white versus black. Kantian philosophy and subjectivity are at the heart of postmodernism.

LESSON 4

THE WEALTH OF NATIONS
Assignment

Why was the concept of laissez-faire so important to the development of the modern nation?

Answer: The concept of laissez-faire was a perfect foil to mercantilism and other forms of state control that contradicted the emerging Protestant state that encouraged individual freedom and initiative. It was astounding to many 18th-century Europeans and Americans that self-interest could actually advance the well-being of nation and individual alike.

Timeline (25 points)

Place the following events in the right order:

2   Louis XVI reigns.

5   Napoleon is proclaimed emperor.

4   Robespierre rules.

3   The Bastille is stormed.

1   The French and Indian War is fought.

Matching (25 points)

C   Storming of the Bastille

A   Guillotine

B   Robespierre

E   Marie Antoinette

D   Committee of Safety

A.   Instrument used to execute condemned persons.

B.   One of the leaders during the Reign of Terror.

C.   Beginning of the French Revolution.

D.   Legislative branch during the Reign of Terror.

E.   Wife of Louis XVI.

Discussion Question (50 points)

Dr. Joseph Ignace Guillotin was a humane man with an idea to lessen the pain of the condemned. Because France had no official means of capital punishment, several popular methods during the Revolutionary period included hanging, often from street lampposts; burning at the stake, used for Joan of Arc's untimely demise; quartering—tying the condemned to four wild horses and sending them galloping off in opposite directions; and other torturous acts. Seeking to end all this, Dr. Guillotin decided that France should be consistent in its means of capital punishment, and that the accepted means should be by swift decapitation. He designed a machine to do it. Do you think the guillotine was the most humane form of punishment? How do you feel about capital punishment in general?

Answer: Answers will vary. There are many committed Christians who support, and oppose, capital punishment. Certainly the guillotine was as humane a way to execute criminals as anything else.

Chapter 26

NATIONALISM

First Thoughts . . .

A "nation-state" was a country whose territory had defined borders and whose principally similar ethnic people were organized by either race or cultural background. Generally in a nation-state, everyone spoke the same language and shared the same set of cultural values. During the period from 1820 to 1871, nation-states achieved mature status in Europe. Nationalism clearly became the basis for the organization of Western civilization. This development not only ended the last vestiges of feudalism, but also set the stage for the replacement of religious wars by national political wars that proved costly and devastating to the Western world.

Chapter Learning Objectives . . .

As a result of this chapter you should be able to:

1. Analyze the rise of nationalism in Europe.
    Answer Assignment 1, chapter Exam: Matching

2. Evaluate the 1848 revolutions that wracked Europe.
    Answer Questions 2-A, 2-B, 2-C

3. Discuss the warring world views that emerged in Europe during this period.
    Answer Assignment Questions 3-A, 3-B, 3-C, Assignment 4

4. Investigate the inevitable rise of Absolutism out of Nationalism.
    Answer Chapter Exam: Discussion Question1

THE RISE OF NATIONALISM

Assignment

Nationalism involves a strong identification of society and the state. Often, it is the belief that an ethnic group has a right to statehood, or that citizenship in a state should be limited to one ethnic group. It can also include the belief that the state is of primary importance, or the belief that one state is naturally superior to all other states. It is also used to describe a movement to establish or protect a homeland (usually an autonomous state) for an ethnic group. In some cases the identification of a national culture is combined with a negative view of other races or cultures. Nationalism is sometimes reactionary, calling for a return to a national past, and sometimes for the expulsion of foreigners. Other forms of nationalism are revolutionary, calling for the establishment of an independent state as a homeland for an ethnic underclass.

Given the above definition, how can Christians, who are first and foremost "citizens of heaven," participate in an earthly national state?

Answer: Christians must put the Kingdom of God first. But, beyond that, they are also citizens of earthly kingdoms. To that degree to which they can participate in the political process without violating their consciences, they should participate.

THE REVOLUTION OF 1848

Assignment

A. The Revolution of 1848 was an international event and, apart from the world wars, the only such event in the West. But it did not affect all of Europe. At least two states, England and Russia, were unaffected. What made these two countries different from the others?

Answer: England was prospering in the Industrial Revolution, and besides, it had a political system that allowed dissenting minorities to have a political voice. Russia was still laboring under feudalism and was ruled by an autocratic despot. There were also so many ethnic minorities it was difficult for a consensus to emerge.

B. The Manifesto of the Communist Party was drafted as its party program by Karl Marx and Frederick Engels in Brussels at the order of the second congress of the League of Communists in December 2–8, 1847. In this document, Marx and Engels argued that European nations were dominated by selfish rulers called bourgeois who dominated the workers or proletariat. In their opinion, only revolution would make things right. To many Europeans the revolutions of 1848 appeared to confirm many of the conclusions offered in the Manifesto. Why?

Answer: Tied to nationalism was an empowering of the ordinary work and citizen. Mark and Engels argued that this empowerment was inevitable. Likewise, the fact that there was so much conflict in Europe confirmed the Marxist view that society was involved in an endless struggle between the proletariat/workers and bourgeois/owners.

C. By 1848 there was a definite propensity in Europe to solve problems through revolutions. Memories of the French Revolution caused people to look again to the mass rally to change governments. Revolutions in 1848 spoke its language, used its symbols, idealized its heroes, and even copied its institutions. However, as Karl Marx argued: "The 1848 Revolution could do no better than parody either 1789, or the revolutionary tradition from 1793 to 1795." In what ways were the European revolutions of 1848 different from the French Revolution?

Answer: Thankfully, no 1848 revolution was so bloody and long. Also, the 1848 revolutions did not lead to the emergence of a Napoleon Bonaparte. Finally, there was very little ideology attached to the nationalist movement—no Rousseau figure wrote to support the Nationalistic movement.

LESSON 3

HEGEL, MARX, AND PROUDHON
Assignment

A. While Hegel was certainly no Christian, his view of "maturity and truth emerging from a struggle" would be appealing to a Christian. Why?

Answer: As illustrated in the life of Jacob, whose name in Hebrew means "struggle," Christians experience internal conflicts throughout their lives. Surely it is not easy to walk the walk every single day. As Paul explains, believers do things they should not do, do not wish to do (Romans 6). However, the struggle is more than mitigated by the joy of walking with God. Christians struggle with the firm assurance that all things work for the good of those called according to His purposes (Romans 8).

B. Clearly, Marx was a determinist Hegelian. What is that?

Answer: Progress came as a struggle ensued between the classes.

C. Proudhon was the father of Absurdism. Explain.

Answer: The "Absurd," in philosophy, refers to the clash between the human tendency to seek inherent meaning and the human inability to find any. As one philosopher explained, "The universe and the human mind do not each separately cause the Absurd, but rather, the Absurd arises by the contradictory reality caused by the confrontation of both, simultaneously." Proudhon was the antithesis of romanticism that celebrated the subjective.

LESSON 4

A RUSSIAN ZIONIST MAKES THE CASE FOR A JEWISH HOMELAND
Assignment

Most people would reject the notion of a "Christian homeland" or a "Buddhist homeland." Are you persuaded that there is a need for a Jewish homeland? Why or why not?

Answer: Perhaps no ethnic or religious group has known more systematic prejudice than the Jewish people. Ninteenth-century Jews, especially Russian Jews, perhaps had more reason than most to desire a new, completely new, homeland. "If we would have a secure home, give up our endless life of wandering and rise to the dignity of a nation in our own eyes and in the eyes of the world, we must, above all, not dream of restoring ancient Judaea. We must not attach ourselves to the place where our political life was once violently interrupted and destroyed. The goal of our present endeavors must be not the 'Holy Land,' but a land of our own."

Matching (30 Points)

D 1. Germany
B 2. France
A 3. Italy
E 4. Austria
C 5. Russia

A. Garibaldi
B. Napoleon III
C. The Romanovs
D. Otto von Bismarck
E. Franz Joseph

Discussion Questions (35 Points Each)

A. Between 1815 and 1848, population growth, commercial or industrial progress, urbanization, and national feeling developed along parallel lines in every European country, reinforcing democratic and nationalistic ideas. The strange thing is that the same demographic movement and the same accelerated economic progress did not continue to produce the same effects during the second half of the century. While France continued to advance democratically, Germany became autocratic, taking an opposite course to that of the Western democracies. Why? Offer an explanation based on your opinion, not on further research. Defend your answer.

Answer: German nationalism evolved into a virulent imperialism that ultimately led to World War I. Why? At the heart of German nationalism was Prussian militarism that produced a militant nationalism that became part of the German political DNA. The German military heritage was epitomized by a succession of Prussian rulers in the 17th and 18th centuries. The first of these was the Great Elector, Frederick William (r. 1640–88), who recognized that a standing army with an elite officer corps was the key to the development of a powerful state in his remote part of the empire. His grandson, Frederick William I (r. 1713–40), more than doubled the size of his professional army to 90,000 and added a trained reserve of conscripted peasants, forming one of the most modern and efficient fighting units in 18th-century Europe. Heavy taxes supported the army, which consumed 80 percent of state revenues even in peacetime. The next Prussian king, Frederick II (r. 1740–86) increased the army to 150,000 and launched a series of wars between 1740 and 1763, wresting control of the province of Silesia from Habsburg Austria. Prussia had become one of the most powerful continental states and a contender with the Habsburgs for domination over the myriad German political entities. The aristocratic character of the officer corps was established early in the 18th century as Prussian kings tried to gain the support of wealthy landed aristocrats, known as Junkers, by granting them a virtual monopoly over the selection of officers. In 1733 a cadet school was established in Berlin to train sons of Junkers to be officers. The officer corps was well on the way to becoming the most privileged social class in Prussia.

B. Negative feelings toward absolutism originated in the spread of the philosophical system of German idealism by Schelling and Hegel. Both men regarded the central philosophical problem of all of history to be the question of the appearance in history of the "absolute" (God, the absolute substance). It bothered them that a divine being would establish a moral system that absolutely must be followed. They preferred the warm levity of "situational ethics" in which nothing is absolute, meaning that an individual's desire is what really matters. How must all Christians respond to this philosophical position?

Answer: Hegel and Schelling, in their belief in the dialectic, or conflicting arguments, understood that there was an absolute power present in the universe. This "power" was a sort of ubiquitous, no-nonsense, judge/creator. However, in spite of that fact, they argued that human behavior—morality—inevitably rises out of compromise, debate, and conflict. Even if that is true, however, Hegel and Schelling should understand that God's law is above man's law. The wages of sin is death! Situational ethics aside, one does not break God's law—God's law breaks the person!

Chapter 27

THE RUSSIAN REVOLUTION

First Thoughts . . .

"The Bolsheviks slavishly imitated speech and gesture of the French Jacobins, just as the Jacobins in turn had imitated the heroes of ancient Rome. But they forgot that the French Revolution itself was drowned in bloody defeat precisely because of its terrorism" (Minister of Justice). The Russian Revolution of 1917 is also called the Bolshevik Revolution or the October Revolution. In 1917 there were actually two revolutions in Russia. One was the February Revolution in which the czar abdicated his throne and the Provisional Government took power. The other was the October Revolution in which the Provisional government was overthrown by the Bolsheviks.

Chapter Learning Objectives . . .

As a result of this chapter you should be able to:

1. Judge the effectiveness and success of the Russian Revolution.
    Answer Question 1

2. Evaluate if the violence engendered in the Russian Revolution was necessary.
    Answer Question 2

3. Trace the events of 1917 that precipitated the October Revolution.
    Answer Assignment 3

4. Assess the impact of Beauvoir's writings on history.
    Answer Assignment 4

5. Discuss what impact Dewey's philosophy had on American education.
    Answer chapter Exam

PRE-REVOLUTIONARY RUSSIA

Assignment

From its inception, why was the Russian Revolution doomed to fail to meet its goals to empower the masses?

Answer: The Revolution had a liberal, faulty view of mankind, that mankind unshackled from control would live peacefully and harmoniously in society. In fact, depraved mankind needs the structure and control of human government, as the Bolsheviks learned quickly and, in fact, created a totalitarian regime more repressive than the czar's government.

THE REVOLUTION UNFOLDS

Assignment

A. The Bolshevik policy of Red Terror promoted the use of mass execution and fear as a tactic to be implemented ruthlessly. Acts of violence were glorified. Latsis, the head of the infamous Cheka (secret police), wrote, "In civil war there are no courts of law for the enemy. It is a life or death struggle. If you do not kill, you will be killed. Therefore kill, that you may not be killed." The Bolsheviks argued that the terror and violence they practiced was necessary, and that the results justified the means. Were they correct?

Answer: One never overcomes evil with evil. From its inception, the Russian Revolution, whose underpinnings were based on the Enlightenment—not the Protestant Reformation—took a violent turn. Ultimately, its utilitarian, gratuitous, excessive violence ended its jaded existence.

B. Trace the events of 1917 that precipitated the October Revolution.

Answer: As World War I grew more violent, and bloody, the unemployed, hungry masses—led by the middle class—rose in revolt in March 1917. The czar abdicated and a representative democracy—provisional democracy—was established. Ultimately this failed in October 1917 when the Bolsheviks took over Russia.

ALEXANDER KERENSKY

Assignment

Some see the Russian Revolution as a long overdue victory for the masses. They argue that it created a grassroots democracy that transformed the workplace and improved the condition of all workers everywhere. Others see the Russian Revolution as an unmitigated disaster, an orgy of bloodthirsty murder and violence against humanity. Who is correct?

Answer: Kerensky recognized the dangers of Communism and tried to find a balance in his Provisional Government. However, the ruthless force of the revolutionaries subjected many to the horrors of rule without godly principles to guide a nation.

LESSON 4
BEAUVOIR AND DEWEY
Assignment

A. Many people feel that Beauvoir was the mother of feminism. What is the basic flaw of feminism?

Answer: While men and women are equal in relationship to God, and while society has no doubt been prejudiced—at times—against women, in fact men and women are different and should assume different roles. Besides, marriage is a liberating experience to all involved—especially to Christians.

B. Why did Dewey's philosophy have such a devastating effect on American education?

Answer: While Dewey's student-centered educational theory has its merits, generally speaking, Dewey replaced a "God" centered educational theory with a "man" centered educational theory. Ironically, putting God at the center of education keeps mankind at the center too—since mankind is created in the image of God and putting God first always brings good things to humankind. His (God's) removal has created havoc in American education.

EXAM KEY

Dates (25 points)

Mark these events in the order they occurred:

1   World War I begins
3   Czar Nicholas II abdicates
2   March Revolution
5   Russian Civil War ends
4   October Revolution

Matching (50 points)

A.	Bolsheviks	E.	Proletariat
B.	Lenin	F.	Nicholas II
C.	Trotsky	G.	Rasputin
D.	White Russians	H.	March Revolution

G   1.   Controversial spiritualist who had a great impact on Russia's royal family.

B   2.   The main leader of the Bolsheviks.

F   3.   Last czar of Russia.

D   4.   Monarchists who opposed the Revolution.

E   5.   A term describing the economic social group from which revolution supposedly would evolve.

C   6.   One of the other leaders; the administrative genius behind Bolshevism.

H   7.   The first revolution that led to a representative democracy.

A   8.   The Communist political party that took over Russia in 1917 during the Russian Revolution.

Essay Question: 60-100 Words (25 points)

Agree or disagree with the following statement: "For one of the first times in history, a grassroots democracy emerged that transformed the workplace and abolished the typical lot of all workers everywhere: having to obey orders, having to accept an authoritarian workplace. Workers and peasants saw that democracy should not be limited to just a parliament and politicians. Instead they saw themselves and their own areas and places of work as the primary locations of democracy. This was where they started the revolution and this was a first in world history—an enormous achievement by ordinary people who had hitherto been confined to the most passive and backward of roles."

Answer: This statement was from an anarchist (someone who prefers no government). Not only did the Russian Revolution fail to free the masses (it in fact enslaved them), it also never brought Russia into the prosperity Bolshevism promised. When the Soviet Union collapsed in the 1990s it was a sick, second-rate power whose people were desperately in need of change.

Chapter 28

GERMAN HISTORY

First Thoughts . . .

While America was developing its nascent democracy, Germany was flirting with despotism. Many people who grew up in the early- to mid-20th century vividly remembered Germany's role in World War I, its enthusiastic acceptance of Nazi rule in 1932, and its despicable role in the Holocaust—the systematic extermination of six million Jews before and during World War II. But that is not the Germany we meet in previous centuries. While always dominated politically by militaristic regimes, Germany nonetheless birthed Beethoven, Bach, Schiller, and Goethe. In fact, it was perhaps the most sophisticated nation on the face of the earth in the mid-20th century. How did this humane, civilized country become so inhumane during the mid-1900s? How much responsibility must be borne by the heroic leader Otto von Bismarck? After the defeat of the Weimar experiment, did the catastrophic defeat of Nazi Germany in 1939–45 finally put the nation back on the track of democratic and humanitarian values?

Chapter Learning Objectives . . .

As a result of this chapter you should be able to:

1. Evaluate what is distinctive about the Germanic culture.
   Answer Assignment 1

2. Discuss the impact of Charlemagne on history.
   Answer Assignment 2

3. Explain how Frederick the Great hindered German unification.
   Answer Assignment 3

4. Explain how Bismarck created the first unified German nation.
   Answer Assignment 4

5. Explain how Germany, the nation that produced Schiller, Goethe, Bach, and Beethoven, could also have produced Hitler, Eichmann, Heydrich, and others who started World War II and created the Holocaust.
   Answer Chapter Exam

THE GERMAN PEOPLE

Assignment

Who were the Germans and what distinctives did they bring to Central Europe?

Answer: The concept of Germany as a distinct region in central Europe can be traced to Roman commander Julius Caesar, who referred to the unconquered area east of the Rhine as Germania, thus distinguishing it from Gaul (France), which he had conquered. This was a geographic expression, as the area included both Germanic tribes and Celts. The victory of the Germanic tribes in the Battle of the Teutonburg Forest (AD 9) prevented annexation by the Roman Empire. Following the fall of the Roman Empire, the Franks subdued the other West Germanic tribes. When the Frankish Empire was divided among Charlemagne's heirs in 843, the eastern part (former Western Germany) became East Francia, ruled by Louis the German. Henry the Fowler became the first king of Germany in 919. In 962, Henry's son Otto I became the first emperor of what historians refer to as the Holy Roman Empire, the medieval German state, with its strong base in Christianity (Internet). From the beginning, Germanic people were fierce warriors, intensely nationalistic, and innovative.

CHARLEMAGNE

Assignment

Summarize Charlemagne's rise to power in the early Middle Ages.

Answer: Charlemagne was king of the Franks (France and parts of Germany) from 768 and emperor of the Holy Roman Empire from 800 to his death. He expanded the Frankish kingdom into an empire that incorporated much of Western and Central Europe. During his reign, he conquered Italy and was crowned Imperator Augustus by Pope Leo III on December 25, 800. This temporarily made him a rival of the Byzantine emperor in Constantinople. His rule is also associated with a revival of art, religion, and culture through the Catholic Church. Through his foreign conquests and internal reforms, Charlemagne helped define both Western Europe and the Middle Ages.

FREDERICK THE GREAT

Assignment

How did Frederick the Great hinder German unification?

Answer: Frederick the Great, a reluctant, right-brain king who loved reading plays more than governing a nascent German Empire, did not desire to see the German states unified under his leadership. He sensed that the more powerful Austrian Empire would not allow it to happen, and he did not want to tempt his neighbor to invade the fragile but growing German states. Frederick knew that some day Germany would conquer Austria, and so it did in 1936.

LESSON 4

OTTO VON BISMARCK

Assignment

Why was Bismarck the perfect politician to unify the German states?

Answer: As prime minister of Prussia from 1862–1890, he oversaw the unification of Germany. He designed the German Empire in 1871, becoming its first Chancellor and dominating its affairs until his dismissal in 1890. His powerful rule gained him the nickname "the Iron Chancellor." After his death, German nationalists made Bismarck their hero, building hundreds of monuments glorifying the symbol of powerful, personal leadership. Historians praised him as a statesman of moderation and balance who was primarily responsible for the unification of the German states into a nation-state. He used balance-of-power diplomacy to keep Europe peaceful in the 1870s and 1880s. He created a new nation with a progressive social policy, a result that went beyond his initial goals as a practitioner of power politics in Prussia. Bismarck, a devout Lutheran who was obedient to his king, promoted government through a strong, well-trained bureaucracy with a hereditary monarchy at the top.

EXAM KEY

Discussion Questions (100 points)

Germany, the nation of Schiller, Goethe, and Beethoven, also produced Hitler, Eichmann, Heydrich, and others who created the Holocaust. How could the most advanced nation in Europe allow the Holocaust to happen?

Answer: Answers will vary. This is a difficult question but an important one. One of the most disturbing essays I have ever read is an essay by Thomas Merton entitled "A Devout Meditation in Memory of Adolf Eichmann." "One of the most disturbing facts," Merton begins, "that came out in the Eichmann trial was that a psychiatrist examined him and pronounced him perfectly sane." The fact is, given our world, we can no longer assume that because a person is "sane" or "adjusted" that he/she is ok. Merton reminds us that such people can be well adjusted even in hell itself! "The whole concept of sanity in a society where spiritual values have lost their meaning is itself meaningless." The central symbol for every 21st-century Christian must be the Cross. At least from the second century onwards, Christians used the Cross as their central symbol. I yearn, as Dietrich Bonhoeffer did at the end of his life, for the crucified Lord to return again—as the rediscovered center—to the center of the Church and American society. America does not need a new religion; it needs Jesus Christ—crucified and resurrected.

Chapter 29

CENTRAL AND SOUTH AMERICAN HISTORY

First Thoughts . . .

Beginning in the 16th century, on another continent, the people and natural resources of South America were repeatedly exploited by foreign conquistadors, first from Spain and later from Portugal. These competing colonial nations claimed the land and resources as their own and divided the land into colonies. European infectious diseases (smallpox, influenza, measles, and typhus)—to which the native populations had no immune resistance—and systems of forced labor decimated the native population. At the same time, Spain was committed to converting their native subjects to Christianity, and was quick to purge any native cultural practices that hindered this goal. Eventually, South America and, later, Central America gained their independence. Today many troubling issues still plague our neighbors to the south!

Chapter Learning Objectives . . .

As a result of this chapter you should be able to:

1. Compare and contrast the Aztecs, Mayas, and Incas.
   Answer Assignment 1

2. Discuss the legacy Spain and Portugal deposited in the New World.
   Answer Assignment 2

3. Explain why Bolivar and other leaders were unable to create a large confederation of South American states.
   Answer Assignment 3

4. Evaluate whether Jim Elliot was inspired or reckless when he flew into the jungle to share Christ with the violent Huaorani people.
   Answer Assignment 4

5. Speculate upon how progress can be balanced with indigenous peoples' needs.
   Answer Chapter Exam A

6. Consider ways Americans can deal with illegal immigration.
   Answer Chapter Exam B

LESSON 1

NATIVE AMERICANS

Assignment

What were some Native American stereotypes shared by many Europeans?

Answer: Europeans loved to stereotype the Native Americans. Many Europeans regarded the Native Americans as immoral and free of all of civilization's restraints. They were wild men and women and certainly inferior to Europeans. Surprisingly, there was a contradictory stereotype too. According to this stereotype, the Native Americans embodied innocence and freedom, lacking private property, yet possessing health and eternal youth. But if some Europeans regarded Native Americans with fascination, most looked at them with fear. The "bloodthirsty savage" who stood in the way of progress and civilization was the stereotype of choice.

LESSON 2

EUROPEAN SETTLERS

Assignment

What legacy did Spain and Portugal deposit in the New World?

Answer: Both the Spanish and Portuguese sought to proselytize the Native Americans. If, however, that was not possible, they destroyed them. They were mercantilists, which meant they sought to take whatever resources they needed from their colonial countries to benefit the mother country, no matter what impact this brought on the natives. Their diseases destroyed native peoples. In other words, the legacy was a tragic one indeed.

LESSON 3

SOUTH AMERICAN INDEPENDENCE

Assignment

Why were Bolivar and other leaders unable to create a large confederation of South American states?

Answer: The socio-economic and cultural differences among South American people groups were much greater than any national or political unifying factors.

LESSON 4

JIM ELLIOT

Assignment

Was Elliot inspired or reckless when he flew into the jungle to share Christ with the violent Huaorani people?

Answer: This author can only repeat the words of Jim Elliot: "He is no fool who gives what he cannot keep to gain that which he cannot lose."

Questions: 60-100 Words (50 points each)

A. A mega-pipeline in South America that would transport gas across the Amazon to other ecosystems is being drowned in criticism in Brazil, where many say the project will destroy the Amazon rainforest. Yet, everyone agrees that the pipeline will bring much-needed improvements to native peoples. Proponents of the pipeline argue, "What are a few rainforest trees compared with several thousand lives?" What do you think?

Answer: The destruction of the rainforest could destroy the ecosystem of the entire world. Is a compromise possible? Can attention be given to rebuilding the rainforest?

B. There are millions of illegal Central American and South American immigrants in the United States. Some states are so frustrated that they are "profiling" potential illegal immigrants. What is profiling, and is it appropriate? If so, when? If not, why?

Answer: The U.S. Immigration Service states, "Illegal immigration continues to be a controversial and divisive topic, not only in the United States, but throughout the world." An individual who is residing in a country illegally is known as an "illegal immigrant." Other terms that are commonly used include: undocumented immigrant, illegal immigrant, undocumented alien, unauthorized migrant, illegal migrant, illegal alien, migrant, or undocumented worker. Illegal immigrants comprise a vast category. Some undocumented immigrants entered the country illegally and others entered legally but overstayed the number of days permitted on their visa or violated the terms of their permanent resident card or refugee permit. Regardless of how a migrant got to their new home country, they decided to take a risk and move to a foreign country in search of a better life. Many usually leave loved ones and valuable possessions behind. Some immigrants leave their home country due to political or economic reasons. Individuals generally choose to emigrate to countries that are more technologically advanced, have greater resources, and offer more opportunities. Some immigrants also move to a foreign country to give their children a better life. In countries like the United States, children of illegal immigrants automatically gain citizenship. On the other hand, in other countries such as France, children are not granted automatic citizenship. Instead, they must request citizenship from the government and fill out applicable documentation once they reach the age of 18. Failure to do so may result in illegal status and deportation. Racial profiling refers to the use of an individual's race or ethnicity by law enforcement personnel as a key factor in deciding whether to engage in enforcement (e.g., make a traffic stop or arrest). The practice is illegal.

Chapter 30

SCANDINAVIAN HISTORY

First Thoughts . . .

Five hundred years before Columbus discovered South America, Vikings, Scandinavians, discovered North America. Though marked by certain geographical, linguistic, and cultural differences, Denmark, Iceland, Norway, and Sweden are united by a common bond and a shared history. They share religions, historical events, political ideas, economic practices, intellectual movements, and technological innovations that have made them what they are. For one thing, they share the Vikings—a most enigmatic people group that, while being notoriously aggressive and ruthless, also practiced the first serious democracy in Northern Europe. Essentially a prehistoric culture, Scandinavians created one of the most effective and enduring legal systems in world history.

Chapter Learning Objectives . . .

As a result of this chapter you should be able to:

1. Speculate as to why the Vikings were so successful in their initial subjugation of cultures in Northern Europe but ultimately failed to have a lasting cultural impact.
   Answer Assignment 1

2. Compare the Vikings' democracy with the ancient Greek democracy in Athens.
   Answer Assignment 2-A

3. Explain how prehistoric Viking society was able to sustain a democracy.
   Answer Assignment 2-B

4. Contrast Scandinavian history with German history.
   Answer Assignment 3

5. Contemplate upon the future of Scandinavia.
   Answer Assignment 4

6. Review Scandinavian history.
   Answer Chapter Exam A, B, C

Assignment

Scandinavian countries, with very few historical exceptions, have cooperated together in common causes to bring peace and harmony. Historians have emphasized the common heritage and geographical similarities that the Scandinavian countries share as possible causes. Yet, China and Japan share a common heritage and geography but they are mortal enemies. Germany and France both emerged from the Holy Roman Empire and the Charlemagne Empire before that. Yet they fought war after war in the 19th and 20th centuries. Why are Scandinavians different?

Answer: There is no sufficient, clear-cut explanation except that these nations, in their isolation, have not been on the path of conquest for any other conqueror. With the exception of Denmark, they lay on the edge of both the 19th-century Napoleonic Empire and the 20th-century German Empire. Frankly, they were not worth the effort to conquer! Reluctantly Germany conquered Norway in World War II to keep Great Britain from doing the same but never considered attacking iron ore–rich Sweden. This geographic isolation and common languages and customs, combined with the peculiarities of history, has given Scandinavia an unequalled time of cooperation and peace among themselves.

Assignment

Viking society was prehistoric (lacking writing and reading). How can a society flourish without reading and writing?

Answer: Answers will vary. They may include the following elements: In an oral culture, the unity and strength is based on corporate identity, often nourished through shared traditions passed on from generation to generation, as well as a sense of personhood that is taught to children through example and societal activities.

Assignment

Contrast the national development of Denmark and Norway with that of Germany. Why were these Scandinavian countries able to stay neutral for so many years?

Answer: Both countries are relatively isolated and unified. They had no temptation to participate in nation building since they were so isolated from the rest of Europe.

BRIEF OVERVIEW OF EACH NATION: PART TWO

Assignment

Speculate upon the future of Scandinavia.

Answer: Answers will vary. Scandinavian countries are very prosperous. They are highly developed democracies with incredibly effective governments. They are historically neutral and seem to have almost no natural enemies. Therefore, Scandinavia should have a prosperous future.

EXAM KEY

Questions: 60-100 Words

A. The first Viking raid on the British Isles occurred in 793 CE, during the reign of King Beorhtric of Wessex. Simeon of Durham recorded the grim events:

"And they came to the church of Lindisfarne, laid everything waste with grievous plundering, trampled the holy places with polluted feet, dug up the altars and seized all the treasures of the holy church. They killed some of the brothers; some they took away with them in fetters; many they drove out, naked and loaded with insults; and some they drowned in the sea."

Given your knowledge of Scandinavian culture, why were these raiders so ruthless? **(34 points)**

Answer: Viking culture celebrated individualism and bravery and gave no mercy to their enemies. Besides, Viking cultural excesses were not mitigated by the morality of Judeo-Christian faith.

B. Why were Viking women relatively "liberated" compared to women from other European societies? **(33 points)**

Answer: "Liberated" is relative but Viking women were expected to perform all their traditional duties and then be ready to fight like a man.

C. The Vikings were among the cleanest of all Europeans during the Middle Ages. In the summer, bathing could be performed in lakes or streams, or within the bathhouse found on every large farm (much like the Finnish sauna, though tub bathing was also used). In winter, the heated bathhouse would be the primary location for bathing. In Iceland where natural hot springs are common, the naturally heated water was incorporated into the bathhouse. Why do you think a culture where the highest temperature was rarely above 75 degrees was so careful to bathe every day? **(33 points)**

Answer: Answers will vary. Cleanliness, for an unknown reason, was endemic to Scandinavian culture.

Chapter 31

WORLD WAR I: A WORLD TRAGEDY

First Thoughts . . .

World War I is the most difficult war of the 20th century to explain. There was no clear-cut issue, no clear-cut victor. On June 28, 1914, Archduke Francis Ferdinand (heir to the Austrian-Hungarian throne) was assassinated during a visit to Sarajevo. At the time of the assassination, Austria-Hungary and Serbia were involved in a serious dispute. The Austrian-Hungarian government was convinced that Serbia was behind the assassination and used the event as an excuse to crush its enemy. Upon declaration of war a chain reaction began leading most of Europe to war. Most Americans were reluctant to get involved, but powerful forces, including German unlimited submarine warfare, pulled the nation into battle. In 1917 American soldiers had joined Europeans in the trenches of war. When the guns finally quieted, President Wilson launched a campaign for a peace treaty and a new organization that would prevent such a tragedy from ever happening again. It failed and a much worse catastrophe was lurking over the horizon.

Chapter Learning Objectives . . .

As a result of this chapter you should be able to:

1. Discuss the causes of World War I.
   Answer Assignment 1

2. Analyze why casualties were so high in World War I.
   Answer Assignment 2

3. Evaluate how effective the Versailles Treaty was.
   Answer Assignment 3

4. Reflect on how contemporaries handled the horror that was World War I.
   Answer Assignment 4

5. Discuss the culpability of all the participants in World War I.
   Answer Chapter Exam Question A

6. Offer contemporary legacies of World War I.
   Answer Chapter Exam Question B

LESSON 1

OVERVIEW

Assignment

In the midst of so much progress and optimism, how could the tragedy that is World War I occur?

Answer: World War I was indeed a tragedy. An unpopular heir to the Austrian throne, Austrian Ferdinand and his wife were assassinated by an unstable Serbian nationalist. Taking advantage of this tragedy, Austria-Hungary determined to impose its will upon the Balkans. The Germans, supremely confident in their Schlieffen Plan, and with a desire for greater power and international influence, gave Austria-Hungary a blank check to wage war in the Balkans. French desire for revenge against Germany following disastrous defeat in 1871 invited them to join the fray. Finally, Russia's anxiety to restore some semblance of national prestige after almost a decade of civil strife and a battering at the hands of the Japanese military in 1905 brought Russia on the side of lowly Serbia, and what began as a local police action quickly escalated into a world war.

LESSON 2

THE WAR

Assignment

Why were casualties so high during World War I?

Answer: War planned with tactics from the 19th century was fought with weapons such as accurate artillery, machine guns, artillery, tanks, and poison gas. The machine gun, in particular, made every battle a massacre. On the Western Front the armies were evenly matched. Trench warfare became a "war of attrition." It was very much a conflict of numbers and of the industrial resources of the two sides.

LESSON 3

THE AFTERMATH

Assignment

How did the Versailles Treaty cause World War II? What would have been a better treaty?

Answer: The anger and resentment that built up in Nazi Germany—and which was played on by Hitler during his rise to power—had long-term causes that went back to the 1919 Treaty of Versailles. Patriotic Germans had never forgotten their nation's treatment. The Versailles Treaty, of course, was, perhaps not the main cause of World War II, but it was one of the causes. World War II was also caused by a worldwide Depression that caused great unrest in Germany. American General Pershing warned that something like this would occur if the Allies did not conquer Germany, take Berlin. But he was ignored. It would have been better if Germany was defeated completely, and knew it, or a true armistice was negotiated where both the Allies and Central Powers negotiated a fair ending to this tragic war. If the Allies would have implemented Wilson's 14 Points, there would have been a just peace indeed.

CONTEMPORARY ACCOUNTS

Assignment

Pretend that you are the pastor responsible to minister to Mr. Remarque, Ms. La Motte, and Mr. Barlett. What can you say to them to encourage them?

Answer: A lesson all Christians will learn at one time or another: inevitably, we must be broken before we will be blessed. Have you ever tried to hug a stiff kid? Impossible! It is easier to hug a muddy kid or a sticky kid, but a stiff, wooden, rebellious child is the hardest child to love. God is in the business of breaking us so that we will really love Him, and so that He can really bless us. It is easier to love a limp, broken saint than to struggle with a stiff one. I once grew an oak tree from an acorn. I lovingly watered and fertilized it, until it was ready to be transplanted in our front yard. Unfortunately, my loving care had scarcely prepared the little oak tree for the violence of rain storms and the back legs of neighborhood dogs. The oak tree did not last a week. Without brokenness, we are ill-prepared to face the violence we see around us. In World War II London, beautiful flowers, unknown since the great fire in 1666, brought to life by nitrates from the burning bombs—life blossoming out of death; beauty, out of pain; the past from out of the present—grew out of useless, grotesque bomb craters (Sacred Journey, Buechner). Brokenness brings beauty and life where there was once death, hopelessness, and despair, as Calvin Miller explains through his allegory, *The Singer*, "If humankind reaches out to God at all, it is with a broken hand." God will only bless a broken people, a people limp from struggling. God's methods are not always physical; they vary, depending on our particular hang-ups and blind spots. The loss of a job; the loss of a spouse; the humiliation of being passed over for a much-deserved promotion—these are only a few of God's resourceful ways that He graciously uses to break us. No one, no one who has seriously pursued God's will for their lives has escaped brokenness. One of the awful, maybe unjust aspects of unforgivingness is that it consumes the guilty and innocent alike. If we do not forgive, we are strangely drawn into the web of our crime. Bruno Bettleheim, a Jewish psychologist held in Dachau Concentration Camp during WW II, illustrates my point well. No one disagrees that the Jews were treated horribly during the War. They were unjustly brutalized, even exterminated by the Nazi regime. But, in a way, the survivors were left with an awful legacy. The Jewish survivors of the Holocaust, Bettleheim suggest, became no better than their captors. They began to emulate the cruelty of their prison guards; because of unforgiveness, in effect, many of them became as angry, hateful, and sadistic as the ones who once tried to destroy them. Because of unforgivingness, they became the evil influence. We must forgive one another, even if the person who hurt us has not repented. Even if we are completely in the right, even if we are the victim. Christ did. As Francis B. Sayre suggests, "Christ depends upon us to show others what He is truly like. It is an awesome thought. But how better can the knowledge of Christ be gained in a world of men and women imprisoned with human bodies?"

EXAM KEY

Questions: 60-100 Words (50 points each)

A. In fact all parties involved were responsible for World War I. If that is true, discuss how each of these countries were partially at fault for World War I: Germany, Italy, Austria-Hungary, Serbia, Russia, France, England, United States.

Answer: Germany overplayed its hand by giving Austria-Hungary a free hand. It could not win this war. Italy was ambitious without the army or navy to sustain its ambitions. Austria-Hungary was too edgy about Serbia and did not grasp the anachronism of its position. Serbia should never had assassinated the Crown Prince and his wife. Russia should have given more attention to the home front and stayed out of this war. France had no business fighting a war on its own territory over a fourth-rate Balkan country. England, too, miscalculated the impact of its support of its Allies. No one saw what this war would become. Finally, the United States was not without fault. American industrialists made fortunes by selling munitions and products to the Allies, and indirectly to Germany. They sustained a war that might have disappeared on its own steam.

B. What contemporary legacies did World War I bring?

Answer: Heightened nationalism remains and the problems in Serbia and Bosnia remain even today. European power waned after World War I, and the ascendancy of Asia and Africa was assured. Total war was now a reality and would be repeated time and time again in the 20th century. New weapons, and the willingness of war leaders to use them, even if there were civilian causalities, meant that new wars would have even more disastrous results.

Chapter 32

THE JAZZ AGE

First Thoughts . . .

The lifestyles of young men and women in the 1920s were as shocking to their parents as the 1960s "hippie" generation were to post–World War II. In reaction to uncontrollable forces around them, including immigration, a consumer revolution, and Prohibition, Americans sought answers in places once considered out of bounds, both morally and physically. Ellen Welles Page, a young woman writing in *Outlook* magazine in 1922, tried to explain why this was:

> Most of us, under the present system of modern education, are further advanced and more thoroughly developed mentally, physically, and vocationally than were our parents at our age. . . . We have learned to take for granted conveniences, and many luxuries, which not so many years ago were as yet undreamed of. [But] the war tore away our spiritual foundations and challenged our faith. We are struggling to regain our equilibrium. . . . The emotions are frequently in a state of upheaval, struggling with one another for supremacy.

In their attempt to come to terms with their place in this new world, Americans tested their new boundaries with more and more outrageous forms of behavior. Wilder music, faster cars, and shorter skirts were just a few symptoms of this strange postwar era called the Jazz Age.

Chapter Learning Objectives . . .

As a result of this chapter you should be able to:

1. Review the events surrounding the Scopes Trial.
   Answer Assignment 1, Chapter Exam

2. Evaluate the effectiveness of Prohibition.
   Answer Assignment 2-A

3. Understand the rise of the Ku Klux Klan.
   Answer Assignment 2-B, 3

4. Analyze the rise of consumer culture in America.
   Answer Assignment 4

THE SCOPES TRIAL

Assignment

Why did evangelical Christians withdraw from American society after the Scopes Trial?

Answer: The Scopes Trial to many evangelical Christians was the cultural turning point in American history. It was undeniable evidence that the United States had moved dangerously away from its Christian roots. Evangelical Christians knew they were in a culture war. There was a mass exodus from American society as evidenced by the founding of a plethora of evangelical colleges. To the secular world, however, the Scopes Trail symbolized the conflict between science and theology, faith and reason, individual liberty and majority rule. The object of intense publicity, the trial was also a clash between urban sophistication and rural fundamentalism. News reporters excoriated the Christians. As the reader can guess, the evangelical fundamentalists were characterized as the bad guys.

PROHIBITION

Assignment

Was Prohibition a "noble experiment" or a misguided effort to use government to shape morality?

Answer: Alcohol remains a serious cause of death, disability, and domestic abuse. It was not until the 1960s that alcohol consumption levels returned to their pre-Prohibition levels. Today, alcohol is linked each year to more than 23,000 motor vehicle deaths and to more than half the nation's homicides, and is closely linked to domestic violence.

THE CONSUMER ECONOMY

Assignment

A historian observed, "A fundamental shift took place in the American economy during the 1920s. The nation's families spent a declining proportion of their income on necessities—food, clothing, and utilities—and an increasing share on appliances, recreation, and a host of new consumer products. As a result, older industries, such as textiles, railroads, and steel declined, while newer industries, such as appliances, automobiles, aviation, chemicals, entertainment, and processed foods, surged ahead rapidly." Speculate upon the problems of a consumer-driven economy.

Answer: Human needs are material items people need for survival, such as food, clothing, and some form of housing. Human wants are not needs. Unfortunately, many consumers began to define wants as needs. Human wants, then, not needs, are the driving force that stimulates demand for goods and services. This causes excessive resources to be utilized for unimportant wants, and important needs are neglected.

THE KU KLUX KLAN

Assignment

Why did the Klan experience such astronomical growth in the 1920s?

Answer: Contributing to the Klan's growth was a post-war depression in agriculture and the migration of African Americans into Northern cities. To many Americans, the United States was changing in ways that were unacceptable. The Klan was a way for marginalized Americans to gain some control over their future.

EXAM KEY

Questions: 60-100 Words (100 points)

What does the image of Amelia Earhart from the 1930s tell us about the influence of the Jazz Age?

Answer: She seems "liberated." She is wearing male clothing and had become a renowned pilot, which was primarily a male-dominated profession.

Amelia Earhart and Lockheed Electra 10E NR16020 (PD-US).

Chapter 33

WORLD WAR II AND BEYOND

First Thoughts . . .

World War II ushered in a new world order, bringing an end to Hitler's Third Reich, Mussolini's fascist dictatorship in Italy, and an aggressive Japanese empire in the Pacific. For the part it played in the Allies' victory, the United States earned a new powerful and coveted role on the world stage. Americans commonly refer to World War II as "the Good War," a conflict in which the forces of good triumphed over the forces of evil.

Chapter Learning Objectives . . .

As a result of this chapter you should be able to:

1. Identify the causes of World War II.
   Answer Assignment 1

2. Analyze the causes and results of the Holocaust.
   Answer Assignment 2-A, 2-B

3. Discuss the roots of the Cold War and the reasons the Allies ultimately won this conflict.
   Answer Assignment 3

4. Ponder Bonhoeffer's contrasting of cheap grace and costly grace.
   Answer Assignment 4

5. Understand why Germany, firmly in control of Europe in 1940, eventually lost World War II in 1945.
   Answer Chapter Exam A, B

Assignment

What were the causes of World War II?

Answer: There have been very few wars where the villains were so obvious: The Japanese and German desire for world conquest. Even the passage of time has not mitigated the chicanery of these two world powers. One can be ambivalent about the Italians

but not the Nazis and Imperial Japan. Not that they wanted the whole world, but enough of it that they could pursue their chauvinistic visions. America entered the war because the Japanese attacked us. Germany declared war on us.

Assignment

In postmodernism there is no right or wrong, no doctrine. What implications can this have for Christianity?

Answer: There is no doctrine, no objective corpus of truth. There are only stories. Everyone wants to tell his/

her "story." It does not matter what our theology is—what matters is that we tell our stories and listen sympathetically to other stories. There is no objective truth from which to work. Postmodern churches do therapy—no real ministry can occur.

Assignment

Identify trends that are occurring in the modern family.

Answer: Divorce has doubled. Couples are cohabitating before marriage at an alarming rate. The majority

of American children grow up in single families or in blended families. All these problems—and they are problems—are interconnected.

Assignment

In your own words, explain the difference between cheap grace and costly grace.

Answer: Bonhoeffer's most famous work is *The Cost of Discipleship*, first published in 1939. This book is a rigorous exposition and interpretation of the Sermon on the Mount and Matthew 9:35–10:42. Bonhoeffer's major concern is cheap grace. This is grace that has become so watered down that it no

longer resembles the grace of the New Testament, the costly grace of the Gospels. By the phrase cheap grace, Bonhoeffer means the grace that has brought chaos and destruction; it is the intellectual assent to a doctrine without a real transformation in the sinner's life. It is the justification of the sinner without the works that should accompany the new birth. Bonhoeffer says of cheap grace: It is the preaching of forgiveness without requiring repentance, baptism without church discipline, Communion without confession, absolution without personal confession. Cheap grace is grace without discipleship, grace without the Cross, grace without Jesus Christ, living and incarnate. Real grace, in Bonhoeffer's estimation, is a grace that will cost a man his life. It is the grace made dear by the life of Christ that was sacrificed to purchase man's redemption. Cheap grace arose out of man's desire to be saved, but to do so without becoming a disciple. The doctrinal system of the church with its lists of behavioral codes becomes a substitute for the Living Christ, and this cheapens the meaning of discipleship. The true believer must resist cheap grace and enter the life of active discipleship. Faith can no longer mean sitting still and waiting; the Christian must rise and follow Christ.

It is here that Bonhoeffer makes one of his most enduring claims on the life of the true Christian. He writes that "only he who believes is obedient, and only he who is obedient believes." Men have become soft and complacent in cheap grace and are thus cut off from the discovery of the more costly grace of self-sacrifice and personal debasement. Bonhoeffer believed that the teaching of cheap grace was the ruin of more Christians than any commandment of works. Discipleship, for Bonhoeffer, means strict adherence to Christ and His commandments. It is also a strict adherence to Christ as the object of our faith. Bonhoeffer discusses this single-minded obedience in chapter three of *The Cost of Discipleship*. In this chapter, the calls of Levi and Peter are used to illustrate the believer's proper response to the call of Christ and the gospel. The only requirement these men understood was that in each case the call was to rely on Christ's word, and cling to it as offering greater security than all the securities in the world.

EXAM KEY

Questions: 60-100 Words (50 points each)

A. Hitler had strong anti-Semitic sentiment. From April 1933, the Jews were dismissed from public service, the universities, and other professions. In September 1935, the infamous Nuremberg Laws were issued that denied German citizenship to Jewish people and forbade them to marry non-Jews. Gradually, restrictions against the Jews worsened: Their property was confiscated, their personal liberty removed, and their personal safety threatened. Six million Jews perished under Nazi rule during the Second World War. If you were Jewish and you lived in Germany during the rise of Hitler, at what point would you decide to emigrate?

Answer: This is a hard question to answer. One would think that you would leave sooner than later. But Anne Frank's father left Germany, moved to Holland, and his family died anyway. He was a war hero and could not know that Hitler would conquer Holland. After all, Holland was neutral during World War I.

B. Why did Germany, firmly in control of Europe in 1940, eventually lose World War II in 1945?

Answer: Germany lost the war because she invaded Russia and declared war on the United States. She overextended herself.

Chapter 34

SOUTH AFRICA

First Thoughts . . .

If the history of South Africa is in large part one of increasing racial divisiveness, it is also the story of—eventually—a journey through massive obstacles towards the creation, from tremendous diversity, of a single nation whose dream of unity and common purpose is now capable of realization. Like Kumalo in *Cry the Beloved Country*, South Africa suffered deeply. By the end of the novel Kumalo lost a brother, a sister, and a son. But he has gained a daughter-in-law, a nephew, and a grandchild as yet unborn. Once, when much younger, he had considered taking a job that would pay better than the priesthood. But suffering ennobles him. He grows into every bit as much a man of God. Instead of becoming a bitter old man, he acquires the vision to bring real change and hope to his community. Today, apartheid is dead but it exacted a great price on the land. Let us hope that this new generation can face new challenges—like the HIV/AIDS epidemic—and bring lasting and permanent change to the land.

Chapter Learning Objectives . . .

As a result of this chapter you should be able to:

1. Discuss the history of South Africa.
   Answer Assignment 1, Chapter Exam

2. Analyze the impact of the Boer people on South Africa.
   Answer Assignment 2

3. Evaluate the causes of the African HIV/AIDS epidemic.
   Answer Assignment 3

4. Discuss five philosophers who greatly impacted the postmodern world.
   Answer Assignment 4-A, 4-B, 4-C, 4-D, 4-E

LESSON 1

SOUTH AFRICAN HISTORY
Assignment

Why was South Africa slow to attract European colonists?

Answer: Until Europeans found valuable natural resources, they saw no reason to settle in inhospitable South Africa. It was always a place to stop on the way to somewhere else (e.g., India).

LESSON 2

THE AFRICAN SLAVE TRADE
Assignment

Describe the devastation of the African slave trade.

Answer: The African slave trade found people torn violently from their homes, cruelly treated and under nourished, with many dying on the long walks or on the journeys across the sea. Millions were uprooted from their homeland in order to serve as slaves in the Americas.

LESSON 3

AIDS/HIV EPIDEMIC
Assignment

What are the causes and the solution to the African AIDS/HIV epidemic?

Answer: HIV/AIDS is a major public health concern and cause of death in Africa. Although Africa is inhabited by just over 14.7% of the world's population, it is estimated to have more than 88% of people living with HIV and 92% of all AIDS deaths in 2007. The causes of the AIDS epidemic are essentially unknown, but most feel it is related to the lifestyle decisions of millions of Africans. Infidelity in marriage and out of marriage has brought havoc on a society that does not value lifelong partners. Public education and medicinal interventions can bring laudable results.

WITTGENSTEIN AND RUSSELL

Assignment

A. The Christian agrees that the Word is primary. What problems, then, if any, does the Christian have with Wittgenstein's philosophy?

Answer: "If a person could not speak it, it was not real." Wittgenstein was the father of postmodernism. Postmodernism is a philosophy that argues that there is no objective theory of knowledge and truth. This of course flies in the face of the biblical witness.

B. Russell's argument that life is based on empiricism, rationality, quantified truth of any sort, is absurd. Honestly, how does one measure hope? Love? Faith? And what is life without those things?

Answer: The things that matter most cannot be quantified and perhaps not even replicated in a systematic way!

EXAM KEY

Questions: 60-100 Words (100 points)

Alan Paton argued that fear, not hatred, is at the heart of apartheid racism. "The truth is, our civilization is not Christian; it is a tragic compound of great ideal and fearful practice, of loving charity and fearful clutching of possessions." What is this fear and is Paton correct?

Answer: Answers will vary. Typically, people are afraid of something, or someone, they do not know and understand.

CHAPTER EXAMS

Examination instructions: The following pages contain the chapter exams, which are comprised of short questions and answers, essays, diagrams, discussions, matching, true and false, and other basic review formats. The teacher has the option of any of the following in order to assist the students in completing these assignments.

1. The exams can be downloaded from the following website, and used for as many students as are participating in the class: www.nlpg.com/worldhistoryexam

2. The teacher can read aloud the statements and questions in order to have students copy them down on note-paper and turn in once complete.

3. The teacher can type up the questions or freely copy question pages from the teacher's guide to give to the students.

Note that the answers and scores for each question are found within the teacher's guide. There is some subjective grading involved with the essays and other questions that involve a student's expressed opinion. This is expected to be done at the teacher's discretion.

CHAPTER 1

Dates (15 points)

Mark these events in the order in which they occurred:

The Sumerians build a city-state.

The Jews are taken to Babylon as exiles.

The Persians invade Mesopotamia.

The Jews rebuild Jerusalem.

The Babylonians invade Mesopotamia.

Matching (35 points)

Answer:

A. Persians	D. Babylonians	G. King Sargon I
B. Sumerians	E. Marduk	H. King Nebachunezzar
C. King Cyrus	F. Ziggurats	I. Tigris and Euphrates

1. The two rivers around whose fertile soil civilization arose in Mesopotamia.
2. The first people to form a city-state, civilization, in Mesopotamia.
3. Akkadian king who for the first time in Mesopotamian history united Sumer and Akkad.
4. A people group that conquered the Mesopotamia area and built the great city of Babylon.
5. Conquered the Babylonians.
6. The Sumerian temples whose distinctive features were their height and width.
7. The chief Babylonian god.
8. This king conquered Jerusalem.
9. This king conquered Babylon and allowed the exilic Jews to return home.

Discussion Question (50 points)

Zerubbabel, prince of Judah and governor of Jerusalem, born in Babylon during the captivity. He was a direct descendant of King David (see Ezra 2:2; Haggai 1:1). When King Cyrus permitted the captive Jews in Babylon to return to Judah (538? BC), Zerubbabel led the first contingent, numbering some 42,000. Cyrus appointed him (see Haggai 1:14) secular governor of Jerusalem. There he organized the rebuilding of the temple, which had been destroyed in 586 BC by King Nebuchadnezzar. However, many scholars believe that he resigned his post and returned to Babylon. I think this is true, Zerubbabel returned to captivity. What causes godly, hardworking, committed Christians to abandon the work and return to comfortable captivity?

CHAPTER 2

Discussion Question (50 points each)

A. Recently, there has been much debate about whether or not the Ten Commandments should be exhibited in government buildings. State both sides of the argument and offer your own conclusions.

B. Compare Hammurabi's Code with the Ten Commandments.

CHAPTER 3

Questions: 100-150 Words (100 points)

One problem the Jewish exiles encountered in Babylon was "syncretism." Define this term and discuss why it is a problem Christians face all the time.

CHAPTER 4

Timeline (25 points)

Number these events in the right order.

_____Moses led the Hebrews from exile.

_____Amon-Ra was the primary God.

_____Cleopatra was queen

_____Alexander the Great conquered Egypt.

_____Pyramids were first built.

Timeline (75 points)

Discuss the most enduring legacy of Egyptian history.

CHAPTER 5

Discussion Question: 150-200 Words (100 points)

Compare and contrast the following passages quoted from the Egyptian and Hebrew writings.

The following is a quote from an Egyptian text honoring the god Amon-Ra:

Behold, the Osiris Ani, the scribe of the holy offerings of all the gods, saith: Homage to thee, O thou who hast come as Khepera, Khepera the creator of the gods, Thou art seated on thy throne, thou risest up in the sky, illumining thy mother [Nut], thou art seated on thy throne as the king of the gods. [Thy] mother Nut stretcheth out her hands, and performeth an act of homage to thee. The domain of Manu receiveth thee with satisfaction. The goddess Maat embraceth thee at the two seasons of the day. May Ra give glory, and power, and truth-speaking, and the appearance as a living soul so that he may gaze upon Heru-khuti, to the KA of the Osiris the Scribe Ani, who speaketh truth before Osiris, and who saith: Hail, O all ye gods of the House of the Soul, who weigh heaven and earth in a balance, and who give celestial food [to the dead]. Hail, Tatun, [who art] One, thou creator of mortals [and] of the Companies of the Gods of the South and of the North, of the West and of the East, ascribe ye praise to Ra, the lord of heaven, the KING, Life, Strength, and Health, the maker of the gods.

The following passage is Psalm 89:1–18:

I will sing of the LORD's great love forever; with my mouth I will make your faithfulness known through all generations. I will declare that your love stands firm forever, that you established your faithfulness in heaven itself.

You said, "I have made a covenant with my chosen one, I have sworn to David my servant, 'I will establish your line forever and make your throne firm through all generations.'" Selah

The heavens praise your wonders, O LORD , your faithfulness too, in the assembly of the holy ones. For who in the skies above can compare with the LORD? Who is like the LORD among the heavenly beings? In the council of the holy ones God is greatly feared; he is more awesome than all who surround him. Who is like you, LORD God Almighty? You are mighty, LORD, and your faithfulness surrounds you.

You rule over the surging sea; when its waves mount up, you still them. You crushed Rahab like one of the slain; with your strong arm you scattered your enemies. The heavens are yours, and yours also the earth; you founded the world and all that is in it. You created the north and the south; Tabor and Hermon sing for joy at your name. Your arm is endued with power; your hand is strong, your right hand exalted.

Righteousness and justice are the foundation of your throne; love and faithfulness go before you. Blessed are those who have learned to acclaim you, who walk in the light of your presence, LORD . They rejoice in your name all day long; they celebrate your righteousness. For you are their glory and strength, and by your favor you exalt our horn. Indeed, our shield belongs to the LORD, our king to the Holy One of Israel.

CHAPTER 6

Questions: 60-100 Words (50 points each)

A. Professor Anne Mahoney asks, "'Always to be the best and be pre-eminent among the others': this is the heroic code as stated by characters in Homer's *Iliad*. What kind of society is built on such a code? Is this ideal compatible with a participatory democracy, in which every citizen has a voice and a vote? Is there a place for heroes in the world of the city?" Answer her question.

B. Greeks were a fierce warrior people who loved their art and their democracy. As one historian explains, "To the Greeks, what was beautiful was holy; to the Jews, what was holy was beautiful. These views were bound to clash." We see that tension reflected in the apostle Paul's letter to the Corinthians. Read 1 Corinthians 15, and in light of the above quote, and your understanding of Greek culture and history, write an interpretive summary of this biblical chapter.

CHAPTER 7

Essay Question: 100-150 Words (100 points)

Write a short essay describing a typical Athenian citizen. Discuss family life and education. Contrast the lives of free persons with lives of slaves, and lives of women with lives of men.

CHAPTER 8

Essay Question: 100-150 Words (100 points)

Why was the ancient peace-loving, democratic Athenian society so skillful at conducting warfare?

CHAPTER 9

Questions: 60-100 Words (50 points each)

A. Pretend that you live in Athens circa AD 45. You belong to a small house church. You are attempting to explain the Gospel to your Greek neighbors. To what Scriptures will you refer in trying to convince your neighbors?

B. What legacy did Alexander the Great leave to the world?

CHAPTER 10

Map study (30 points)

Identify each of the following places by its letter:

___ Athens

___ Sparta

___ Gulf of Corinth

___ Peloponnesian Penisula

___ Aegean Sea

___ Macedonia

Essay Questions: 60-100 Words (70 points)

A member of a family is tragically killed in an automobile accident. Discuss how each of the following philosophers would explain this terrible event.

A. Plato

B. Aristotle

C. Apostle Paul

CHAPTER 11

Questions: 60-100 Words

A. The historian Edward Gibbon wrote, "The various modes of worship, which prevailed in the Roman World, were all considered by the people as equally true; by the philosopher as equally false; and by the magistrate as equally useful. And thus toleration produced not only mutual indulgence, but even religious accord." Why do you agree or disagree with his assessment? Most of us prefer a society that has a high regard for religious freedom and widespread toleration, but what is the danger that this freedom poses? **(75 points)**

B. Augustine's *City of God* (AD 426), written at the very end of the Roman Empire, purported to prepare Christians to survive and even to prosper in the hostile environment that they would encounter with the collapse of the Roman Empire. If you accept that Christians are now a minority in America, explain how we can prepare to survive and thrive in this inhospitable, post-Christian era. **(25 points)**

CHAPTER 12

Essay Question: 100-150 Words (100 points)

Some scholars compare the ancient Roman Empire to our "American Empire" in the 21st century. What similarities and differences can you identify? In your answer, include discussions about religion, the family, entertainment, and the military.

CHAPTER 13

Matching (50 points)

A. Romulus and Remus
B. Etruscans
C. Punic Wars
D. Hannibal
E. Roman Monarchy
F. Roman Republic
G. Spartacus
H. Julius Caesar
I. Augustus
J. Constantine
K. Goths
L. Roman Empire

_____ 1.   The earliest period of Rome.
_____ 2.   The leader of a great slave rebellion.
_____ 3.   The time of democratic government in Roman history.
_____ 4.   The emperor leading Rome during its golden age.
_____ 5.   Carthaginian leader.
_____ 6.   The emperor who made Christianity the most favored religion.
_____ 7.   A barbarian people who twice attacked Rome and ultimately conquered it.
_____ 8.   The last period of history in which dictators were the authorities in Rome.
_____ 9.   The first Roman emperor.
_____ 10. The first civilization living in the Tiber area where Rome was founded.
_____ 11. Legendary founders of Rome.
_____ 12. Three Roman conflicts with Carthage.

Essay Question: 80-100 Words (50 points)

With virtually no explanation, the author Edith Hamilton finished her book *The Roman Way* with this statement: "Material development outstripped human development." What do you suppose she meant?

Are we living during the end of the "American Empire"? Defend your answer.

CHAPTER 14

Questions: 60-100 Words

A. Mani (216–274) was the founder of Manichaeanism, a religion that argued that matter is intrinsically evil, the prison of the soul. Salvation was through gnosis, an inner illumination in which the soul gained knowledge of god. The righteous went to paradise at death, but the wicked were reborn to live another life. This religion was very popular among intellectuals (e.g., Augustine followed Manichaeanism before his conversion). Why? **(34 points)**

B. Pope Leo I (440–461) exhorted the Church to desist from mixing Christianity with sun worship. For instance, he rebuked his flock for paying reverence to the sun god on the steps of St. Peter's before entering the basilica. How do contemporary Christians mix their faith with other religions? **(33 points)**

C. Heresy is more an excess of good theology than an aberration of bad theology. Explain what this statement means and agree or disagree with it. **(33 points)**

CHAPTER 15

Questions: 60-100 Words

A. Philo was also a theologian who sought to harmonize Jewish theology with Greek (largely Platonic) philosophy. In today's vernacular, Philo tried to make Judaism "modern" by harmonizing it with secularism. Later Christian theologians (e.g., Origen) tried to do the same thing. Is it possible to make the Christian message more "modern" without compromising its integrity? If not, why? If so, how? **(34 points)**

B. The theologian/church father Ignatius claimed that the bishop was God's representative on earth. In a letter to the Ephesians, Ignatius wrote, "Be ye subject to the Bishop and Presbytery. . . . For even Jesus Christ, our inseparable Life, is the manifest Will of the Father; as also Bishops, to the uttermost bounds of the earth, are so by the will of Jesus Christ." In light of the view of the doctrine of the priesthood of all believers (see Rev. 1:4–6), do you agree or disagree with Ignatius? Explain your reasoning **(33 points)**.

C. In AD 127–42, Ptolemy, a committed Christian and astronomer, postulated that the earth was the center of the universe. This view held until 1542, when Copernicus supplied a solar-centered model. While Ptolemy's view seemed to concur with Orthodox Christianity, from the beginning there has been a tension between faith and science. What is this tension and how can it be resolved? **(33 points)**

CHAPTER 16

Questions: 60-100 words (50 points each)

A. In ancient Europe there were several tales such as *Beowulf* and *The Song of Roland* whose heroes were courageous and bold. At the same time, ballads emerged that described the lives of common people (e.g., "The Ballad of Robin Hood"). In contrast, Japanese ballads rarely extolled the lives of common people. On the contrary, Japanese ballads celebrated the exploits of the kings and the deeds of heroes. Why?

B. Roman Catholicism had a great impact on European ancient life. Likewise, Shintoism and Buddhism impacted Japanese life in a different way. How?

CHAPTER 17

Essay Question: 80-100 Words (100 points)

One historian claims that it is impossible to understand Indian history unless one understands Hinduism. Even Christians, they argue, are affected by "Hindi culture." Agree or disagree and give reasons for your opinion.

CHAPTER 18

Essay Question: 80-100 Words (100 points)

There is a Persian Proverb that says, "History is a mirror of the past and a lesson for the present." How does Persian history mirror those words?

CHAPTER 19

Questions: 60-100 words (50 points each)

A. In spite of China's strong beginning, why did European technology quickly surpass Chinese technology?

B. To many ancient Chinese authorities, the arrival of Buddhism from India was perceived as a religious and political threat. Indeed, many Daoist and Legalist Chinese officials saw it as a threat to everything dear in their culture. Today, some Americans are similarly concerned about the growth in America of such religions as Islam, Hinduism, and Buddhism. They are afraid that these religions are a threat to America's unique culture. Explain why you agree or disagree with their assessment.

CHAPTER 20

Questions: 60-100 Words (50 points each)

A. Why is it incorrect to call the Middle Ages the "Dark Ages"?

B. Bubonic Plague started in China and made its way west across Asia to the Black Sea by 1347. One theory is that a group of infected Tartars besieged a Genoese outpost on the coast. To harass the trapped townspeople, the Tartars used their catapults to hurl the dead bodies of their comrades over the town walls, spreading the epidemic among the Genoese. The panicked inhabitants fled the scene by ship, showing up in the ports of northern Italy and bringing the Black Death to Europe. Why was the Bubonic Plague so difficult to contain?

CHAPTER 21

Questions: 60-100 Words

A. In a broad sense, the Crusades were an expression of militant Christianity and European expansion. While the original purpose of the Crusades was religious, it quickly became secular. The Crusades combined religious interests with secular and military enterprises. In many ways this was a disconcerting beginning. Why? **(33 points)**

B. Under what, if any, circumstances should Christians pressure others to embrace the Christian faith? **(33 points)**

C. What impact did the Crusades have on Western Europe? **(34 points)**

CHAPTER 22

Questions: 60-100 Words

A. Why did Portugal lead Europe in the initial stages of exploration? **(25 points)**

B. Discuss how the Crusades stimulated the Age of Discovery. **(25 points)**

C. Why did Europe send explorers east and west to find China, while China conducted no similar explorations? **(50 points)**

CHAPTER 23

Questions: 60-100 Words (50 points each)

A. To our present-day hopeless, secular world, history is mundane; it is merely utilitarian. To Christians, history is sacred, fraught with opportunity. To secular people, history is not didactic; it helps people feel better. To Christians, history is full of important lessons, and it challenges people to be all they can be in Christ. To secular people, time and space are finite entities full of fearful pitfalls. To Christians, no matter how bad things are, because God is alive and well, time is holy and the land is holy. Secular people act out of no purpose or design. In contrast, Christians know that God is in absolute control of history. In a way that is not mawkish or condescending, Christians must be tirelessly hopeful. We can do that by speaking the truth of God's Word in places where truth is not recognized. Cite examples of how modern scholars, politicians, and philosophers are not fully appreciating history.

B. Every generation thinks that it does everything new–that it reinvents the wheel, so to speak. Certainly this was the case with my generation growing up in the 1960s. Compare and contrast your generation with the Renaissance generation.

CHAPTER 24

Questions: 60-100 words

A. As a reporter for a newspaper, write an article on the Protestant Reformation. You are required to include the following topics (**60 points**):

1. Causes of the Reformation

2. Key Figures: Calvin, Wycliffe, Erasmus

3. Similarities and differences between the Roman Catholic Church and the early Protestant Church

4. Results of the Reformation

B. Many Christian scholars, including this author, feel that some Protestant reformers went too far in their protests against the Roman Catholic Church. What happens when a legitimate reform movement tries to overcome poor choices with equally poor ones? (**40 points**)

CHAPTER 25

Timeline (25 points)

Place the following events in the right order

_____Louis XVI reigns.

_____Napoleon is proclaimed emperor.

_____Robespierre rules.

_____The Bastille is stormed.

_____The French and Indian War is fought.

Matching (25 points)

_____Storming of the Bastille

_____Guillotine

_____Robespierre

_____Marie Antoinette

_____Committee of Safety

A. Instrument used to execute condemned persons.

B. One of the leaders during the Reign of Terror.

C. Beginning of the French Revolution.

D. Legislative Branch during the Reign of Terror.

E. Wife of Louis XVI.

Discussion Question (50 points)

Dr. Joseph Ignace Guillotin was a humane man with an idea to lessen the pain of the condemned. Because France had no official means of capital punishment, several popular methods during the Revolutionary period included hanging, often from street lampposts; burning at the stake, used for Joan of Arc's untimely demise; quartering—tying the condemned to four wild horses and sending them galloping off in opposite directions; and other torturous acts. Seeking to end all this, Dr. Guillotin decided that France should be consistent in its means of capital punishment, and that the accepted means should be by swift decapitation. He designed a machine to do it. Do you think the guillotine was the most humane form of punishment? How do you feel about capital punishment in general?

CHAPTER 26

Matching (30 points)

1. ____Germany   A.   Garibaldi

2. ____France   B.   Napoleon III

3. ____Italy   C.   The Romanovs

4. ____Austria   D.   Otto von Bismarck

5. ____Russia   E.   Franz Joseph

Discussion Question (35 points each)

A. Between 1815 and 1848, population growth, commercial or industrial progress, urbanization, and national feeling developed along parallel lines in every European country, reinforcing democratic and nationalistic ideas. The strange thing is that the same demographic movement and the same accelerated economic progress did not continue to produce the same effects during the second half of the century. While France continued to advance democratically, Germany became autocratic, taking an opposite course to that of the Western democracies. Why? Offer an explanation based on your opinion, not on further research. Defend your answer.

B. Negative feelings toward absolutism originated in the spread of the philosophical system of German idealism by Schelling and Hegel. Both men regarded the central philosophical problem of all of history to be the question of the appearance in history of the "absolute" (God, the absolute substance). It bothered them that a divine being would establish a moral system that absolutely must be followed. They preferred the warm levity of "situational ethics" in which nothing is absolute, meaning that an individual's desire is what really matters. How must all Christians respond to this philosophical position?

CHAPTER 27

Dates (25 points)

Mark these events in the order in which they occurred:

___World War I begins

___Czar Nicholas II abdicates

___March Revolution

___Russian Civil War ends

___October Revolution

Matching (50 points)

A. Bolsheviks   E. Proletariat

B. Lenin   F. Nicholas II

C. Trotsky   G. Rasputin

D. White Russians   H. March Revolution

_____ 1. Controversial spiritualist who had a great impact on Russia's royal family.

_____ 2. The main leader of the Bolsheviks.

_____ 3. Last czar of Russia.

_____ 4. Monarchists who opposed the Revolution.

_____ 5. A term describing the economic social group from which revolution supposedly would evolve.

_____ 6. One of the other leaders; the administrative genius behind Bolshevism.

_____ 7. The first revolution that led to a representative democracy.

_____ 8. The Communist political party that took over Russia in 1917 during the Russian Revolution.

Essay Question: 60-100 Words (25 points)

Agree or disagree with the following statement: "For one of the first times in history, a grassroots democracy emerged that transformed the workplace and abolished the typical lot of all workers everywhere: having to obey orders, having to accept an authoritarian workplace. Workers and peasants saw that democracy should not be limited to just a parliament and politicians. Instead they saw themselves and their own areas and places of work as the primary locations of democracy. This was where they started the revolution and this was a first in world history—an enormous achievement by ordinary people who had hitherto been confined to the most passive and backward of roles."

CHAPTER 28

Essay Question: 80-100 Words (100 points)

Germany, the nation of Schiller, Goethe, and Beethoven, also produced Hitler, Eichmann, Heydrich, and others who created the Holocaust. How could the most advanced nation in Europe allow the Holocaust to happen?

CHAPTER 29

Questions: 60-100 Words (50 points each)

A. A mega-pipeline in South America that would transport gas across the Amazon to other ecosystems is being drowned in criticism in Brazil, where many say the project will destroy the Amazon rainforest. Yet, everyone agrees that the pipeline will bring much-needed improvements to native peoples. Proponents of the pipeline argue, "What are a few rainforest trees compared with several thousand lives?" What do you think?

B. There are millions of illegal Central American and South American immigrants in the United States. Some states are so frustrated that they are "profiling" potential illegal immigrants. What is profiling, and is it appropriate? If so, when? If not, why?

CHAPTER 30

Questions: 60-100 Words

A. The first Viking raid on the British Isles occurred in 793 C.E., during the reign of King Beorhtric of Wessex. Simeon of Durham recorded the grim events:

> And they came to the church of Lindisfarne, laid everything waste with grievous plundering, trampled the holy places with polluted feet, dug up the altars and seized all the treasures of the holy church. They killed some of the brothers; some they took away with them in fetters; many they drove out, naked and loaded with insults; and some they drowned in the sea.

Given your knowledge of Scandinavian culture, why were these raiders so ruthless? (**34 points**)

B. Why were Viking women relatively "liberated" compared to women from other European societies? (**33 points**)

C. The Vikings were the among the cleanest of all Europeans during the Middle Ages. In the summer, bathing could be performed in lakes or streams, or within the bathhouse found on every large farm (much like the Finnish sauna, though tub bathing was also used). In winter, the heated bathhouse would be the primary location for bathing. In Iceland where natural hot springs are common, the naturally heated water was incorporated into the bathhouse. Why do you think a culture where the highest temperature was rarely above 75 degrees was so careful to bathe every day? (**33 points**)

CHAPTER 31

Questions: 60-100 Words (50 points each)

A. All parties involved were somewhat responsible for World War I. If that is true, discuss how each of these countries were partially at fault for World War I: Germany, Italy, Austria-Hungary, Serbia, Russia, France, England, United States.

B. What contemporary legacies did World War I bring?

Questions: 60-100 Words (100 points)

What does the image of Amelia Earhart from the 1930s tell us about the influence of the Jazz Age?

Amelia Earhart and Lockheed Electra 10E NR16020 (PD-US).

CHAPTER 33

Questions: 60-100 Words (50 points each)

A. Hitler had strong anti-Semitic sentiment. From April 1933, the Jews were dismissed from public service, the universities, and other professions. In September 1935, the infamous Nuremberg Laws were issued that denied German citizenship to Jewish people and forbade them to marry non-Jews. Gradually, restrictions against the Jews worsened: Their property was confiscated, their personal liberty removed, and their personal safety threatened. Six million Jews perished under Nazi rule during the Second World War. If you were Jewish and you lived in Germany during the rise of Hitler, at what point would you decide to emigrate?

B. Why did Germany, firmly in control of Europe in 1940, eventually lose World War II in 1945?

CHAPTER 34

Questions: 60-100 Words (100 points)

Alan Paton argued that fear, not hatred, is at the heart of apartheid racism. "The truth is, our civilization is not Christian; it is a tragic compound of great ideal and fearful practice, of loving charity and fearful clutching of possessions." What is this fear and is Paton correct?

Your High School History Curriculum

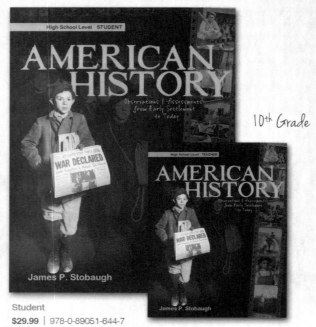

10th Grade

Student
$29.99 | 978-0-89051-644-7

Teacher
$14.99 | 978-0-89051-643-0

11th Grade

Student
$24.99 | 978-0-89051-646-1

Teacher
$14.99 | 978-0-89051-645-4

12th Grade

Student
$24.99 | 978-0-89051-648-5

Teacher
$14.99 | 978-0-89051-647-8

Available where fine books are sold or nlpg.com

follow the Author:

 facebook.com/**JPStobaugh**   **@JamesPStobaugh**   forsuchatimeasthis.com